Date Due

APR 0 9 2013			

COMPLETE GUIDE TO FISHING

Baitfishing

COMPLETE GUIDE TO FISHING

Baitfishing

MASON CREST PUBLISHERS, INC.

COMPLETE GUIDE TO FISHING – **Baitfishing** has been originated, produced and designed by AB Nordbok, Gothenburg, Sweden.

Publisher
Gunnar Stenmar

Editorial chief
Anders Walberg

Design, setting & photowork:
Reproman AB, Gothenburg, Sweden

Translator:
Jon van Leuven

Nordbok would like to express sincere thanks to all persons and companies who have contributed in different ways to the production of this book.

World copyright © 2002
Nordbok International,
P.O.Box 7095,
SE-402 32 Gothenburg, Sweden.

Published in the United States by
Mason Crest Publishers, Inc.
370 Reed Road, Broomall, PA 19008
(866) MCP-BOOK (toll free)
www.masoncrest.com

First printing
1 2 3 4 5 6 7 8 9 10
Library of Congress Cataloging-in-Publication Data on file at the Library of Congress

ISBN 1-59084-494-7

Printed and bound in Jordan 2002

Contents

Preface

One of the fascinating aspects of baitfishing is how the sport has developed differently in various parts of the world. There are sound reasons for the differences, mostly environmental or climatic, but what is becoming more and more appreciated is that everyone can learn something useful from everyone else. Simply by studying the baitfishing magazines of many lands, it is possible for even the nonlinguist to see how ideas and approaches are beginning to travel around this planet.

The history of modern angling

Catching fish with a baited hook is a practice that has certainly existed as long as human beings, but modern angling is usually associated with the age that has given us TV and computers. However, read these quotations:

"Chop up some cat or rabbit meat... mix with bone-meal... or other meal. Add sugar or preferably honey... knead it with the hands. Form... bait balls."

"...throw a bit of the dough into the pond or river where you intend to fish. If you... throw small balls of the dough into the water now and then, a few days beforehand... if the pond is large, you can lure the fish to a particular place, and do your fishing with hopes of success..."

This is modern carp fishing in a nutshell. With a prebaiting strategy and recipes for bait which if boiled, would have been boilies, a high-tech bait for carp. Today's fishermen have only exchanged cat and rabbit meat for milk powder and the like.

The above quotations are from a book, *The Compleat Angler*, which was published in England in 1653. Thus, modern angling has much older roots than most people realize, when they follow a prebaiting strategy for large bream or buy boilies in the store. Izaak Walton, the book's author, came from England, and it is largely the developments in Great Britain that we have to thank for modern angling.

Specimen angling

During the 1950s some fisherman began to go after big carp in the waters of Reedmire, in Wales. Although it was then believed that carp were impossible to catch (Walton's work in the 1600s had been forgotten), these efforts succeeded. The pioneer, Richard Walker, landed a carp of 19.9 kg (44 lb). It was christened Clarissa and became a new English record, lasting until well into the 1970s. Walker and his colleagues established the principles that we see in modern angling directed at large fish – specimen angling. The fish must be handled with respect and released, and today there are many waters in Europe where fish that have been caught several times bear their own names.

The success with carp stimulated directed angling for other species, and soon there were 'specimen groups' all over the country, specializing in pike, bream, eel and so on. These groups experimented freely with bait. During the 1970s the idea arose that paste made of egg and various sorts of flour

could be boiled to produce a bait that was both adored by carp and ignored by smaller fish. A magic ball – the boilie – was born and the carp-fishing boom, which has by now conquered the continent, began.

Equipment

Hunters of huge fish also found that contemporary equipment was not very good, which led to the development of today's modern rods for angling with a reel. The same period also brought refinements in fishing with a rod that has no reel, the 'top knot' angling rod, in countries such as Italy and France. In the wake of the new gear, interest in fishing contests grew, and rods for light float angling have thus acquired the name of 'match rods'. In Italy, competition angling has expanded so far as to become the nation's biggest public sport after football!

Above: Modern angling is a source of enjoyment and relaxation as well as comradeship and ranges from carp fishing to catching predators

Right: In modern angling it is a basic principle that the fish should be treated respectfully and returned to the water

Equipment
Rods
Light float angling

Match rods are made for angling with light floats that carry 0.5–10 grams. (0,17-0,35 oz) In order to be able to cast the tackle of float, sinker and hook, thin lines of 0.10–0.18 mm (0,004-0,007 in) are required. The rods have many rings to prevent the lines from catching against the blade. Their length is around four meters, and the action depends on the kind of fishing. More top action is needed to fish fast for species such as bleak and roach, with rapid response to quick takes a few rod lengths out. Deeper action suits fishing with heavier floats at a greater distance, or for larger fish, since more line has to be lifted when hooking and one must minimize the risk of breaking the line if the fish lunges.

Light bottom angling

Rods for light bottom angling, of about 10–45 g (0,35-1,5 oz), come in two types. A quivertip rod reveals the take at its tip. It has exchangeable tops for different kinds of fish-ing. In strong currents or at great distances, a stiffer top is needed. Close up, and in still waters, the top should be soft-er. Such rods are around 11–12 feet (3.5 m) long. A ledger rod, which is around 10-feet (3 m) long, has a threaded top-ring, where an extra top can be screwed on. It can be fished with a screwed-on quivertip or a swingtip (see Bottom angling).

Heavier bottom and float angling

Rods for heavier bottom angling, of 45–150 g (1,5-5,2 oz), are synonymous with carp rods. However, they are also used for other heavy work such as pike angling. They are classified in pounds, usually 1–3 lbs (0.4–1.3 kg). The fishing distance determines the rod's action and power. Really long casts, over 100 m (330 ft), call for the most power and top action, but are also more risky as the fish may tear loose, especially when near the net. A softer rod with lower class, about 2 lbs (1.Kg), can be considered an all-rounder. It catches up the fish's lunges better, decreas-ing the risk of a line break or of losing the fish by tearing the hook loose.

The rod holder is a prerequisite for effective bottom angling, here with a quivertip rod.

A quivertip rod for bottom angling is up to 12-feet (3.5 m) long and has exchangeable tops with different stiffness.

In the netting phase, the risk is greatest that the fish will be lost if it makes a wild lunge. A weaker rod absorbs the lunge much better than a stiff rod.

Swingers hang by an arm attached to the rod holder or rack. The best models have movable weighs on arms so that the resistance can be adjusted. A swinger holds the line stretched and ensures that line movement (when a fish takes bait) is sensed by the electronic bite indicator so that it bleeps and blinks.

Long rods

A long rod has the line knotted at its top. There are two variants: telescopic rods of fixed lengths from 10–45 feet (3–14 m), which are fished with full line length, and the 'take-apart' rod, which can be disassembled in parts about 5 feet (1.5 m) long. The latter is fished with a short line, about a meter from the rod tip to the float. When the fish bites, the fisherman pulls the rod in until the length of line is sufficient for dividing the rod and lifting in the fish, or drawing it over the net. This rod has a length of 20–50 feet (6–16 m).

Reels

The spinning reel is the angling reel. Special models for light float and bottom angling have extra-shallow spools, so that there is no need for many hundred meters of thin line to fill them to the right depth.

For heavier angling, as in carp fishing, or on the bottom for pike, the most often-used models have a 'baitrunner function' – a button on the reel that can free the spool and enable a fish to pull line. When the button is pressed, a pre-set brake intervenes.

Bite indicators

Apart from the quivertip and swingtip, there are two types of indicators: electronic, with signaling by sound and light, and mechanical. The latter is used in combination with an electronic one, to make it react regardless of whether the fish swims toward or away from the fisherman, and to show clearly which rod the take is on.

Mechanical

With a 'monkey climber' the fisherman can have an open bail on the reel, allowing the fish to pull line without resistance. At the take, the 'monkey' climbs up on the pin, until more line is released from the reel and it slides back down. If the fish swims inward, the 'monkey' falls. A 'swinger' is adapted to fishing with baitrunner reels, and has a weighted arm that hangs on the line near the electronic indicator. A pure 'hanger' indicator is also popular with a baitrunner, but cannot be as nearly weightless on the line as a 'swinger'.

Electronic

Electronic indicators are used in all angling where a long time may pass between bites – for example by carp, sheatfish, pike and tench. They are both rod holders and bite alarms, bleeping and blinking when the line moves. The best kinds have adjustable volume and sensitivity, as well as a light diode that shines for several seconds after the line has moved, so that one can see which rod is involved. Such an aid is essential when fishing for species that bite cautiously, or in carp fishing when smaller fish dart in to pull at the hook bait, so that the fisherman can tell which bait may need to be changed.

Rod supports

Bankstick.
A bankstick is a telescopic 'stick' that serves as a rod holder, alarm and so on.

Rod holder

When fishing without a bite indicator, a rod holder is necessary. It is threaded to screw onto a bankstick. Ideally, the rod can be placed in several positions to find the best one for seeing the take.

Rod rack

For fishing with several rods at once, it is common to use a rack on legs. Both a bite indicator and bite alarm can be kept there. This is invaluable in places where a bankstick cannot be set firmly in the ground.

Nets

A net is indispensable. Smart fishermen always have their net ready and close to hand. The first take can mean a dream fish. And how many times have I myself stood trying to screw the net together with a big carp doing its best to wriggle loose? A good net has a knotless, fine mesh. It is wide and deep enough for a large fish to go in easily. For pike and carp, it must be at least a meter wide, but 60 cm (2 ft) is sufficient to hold a tench or bream, for example.

The monkey climber hangs on a pin with the line locked between itself and the pin. It climbs up when a fish bites, or falls if the fish swims inward. It is perfect for fishing with an open bail, so that the fish can pull line without resistance. Then the monkey climbs until line is released from the spool, slides down and climbs again, and so on.

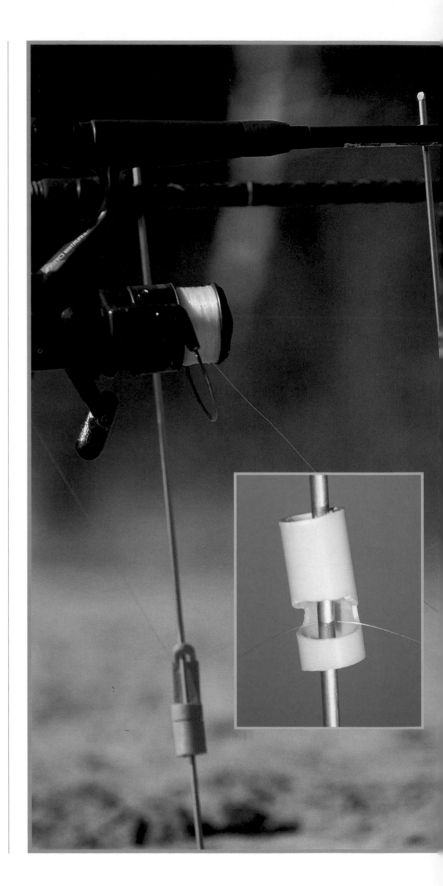

Hook and line

Nylon line in dimensions from about 0.06 to 0.45 mm (0.002-0.02 in), despite the success of braided lines, is the best line for angling, with few exceptions. Hooks come in countless models with special properties. Line dimensions, hook models and sizes are given in the sections on different species.

Other accessories

Also useful in modern angling are scales, to weigh the fish before it is returned, and many other gadgets to make the fishing comfortable. These include special tents, parasols, beds and the like.

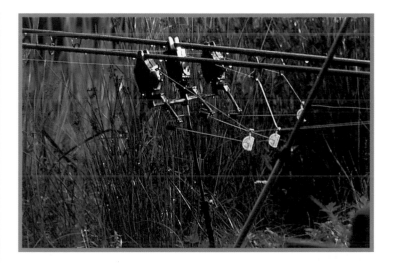

The carp fisherman sits protected from the rain under a parasol, the rods being rigged with bite alarms and indicators so that the slightest movement of line by a fish gives a clear signal in the form of a waving swinger and blinking, bleeping alarm.

Modern angling is often directed at species such as carp, sheatfish, pike and tench, whose bites may occur at long intervals. This has led to the development of electronic alarms and many other aids for the fisherman's comfort – including special tents, parasols and beds.

The net must be able to hold the biggest fish you can imagine biting. For carp and pike, it should be at least a meter wide.

Fish management

Modern angling, with few exceptions, is a matter of catching and releasing the fish. Every caught fish must therefore be treated with care and respect, to be in the same condition when it is returned to the water as before it took the bait. Photographing the fish for posterity commonly precedes the release.

Accessories and handling

Carp fishing has been developed into a kind of art, but all fish should still be handled equally well if they are to be released. What follows here is advice on how to deal with the catch from the moment it is netted until it returns to its natural element. Considerateness starts before the fishing trip. With these accessories and methods, the risk of damaging the fish is minimized.

    Landing net. A net with soft, knotless mesh yarn.

    Carp sack. A keep-sack that the fish can be laid in while, say, waiting for comrades to help with photography, or setting up your own camera. A carp sack is made of soft nylon cloth that lets in water. Fish that are placed inside it will normally stay still and recover.

    Carp rug. A carp rug is a soft 'fish mattress'. It is wetted before laying the fish on it, to protect the fish's slime layer, and prevents damage if the fish thrashes about. The rug is used both when the hook must be removed and when photographing. Generally the fish stays calm if its eyes are covered with, for example, a carp sack. If the fish has spent time in a sack, it will usually have regained strength, so one must be ready for wriggles and leaps. Big fish are held low over the rug to avoid injury, should the fisherman lose his grip. If a large fish such as a carp begins to twist loose, it can be held with a hug, pulling it toward the body and locking your arms round it.

    Really large fish, such as pike of monstrous dimensions, should not be lifted completely if the fisherman is on top. Then it is easier to lift only the pike's head and front body, letting the rest stay lying on the rug. The fish must never be held upright with a grip on the gills or head, as this can damage its internal organs.

Disgorger. A disgorger is for loosening single hooks, and forceps for treble hooks. If the hook is badly stuck in the fish's throat, it can be better to cut the line or leader than to try loos-

A carp sack, made of soft nylon cloth that lets in water, is perfect for storing fish in while waiting for a photo. There they stay still and can recover after the fight.

ening the hook and risk serious bleeding. A large pike is held firmly when laid on its back; the fisherman straddles it and lifts up its head.

Returning the fish

Lower the fish into the water and keep hold of it. Move it carefully back and forth if it seems exhausted, so that fresh water enters its mouth and streams over the gills. Grip it with one hand by the narrow part of the tail and support it with the other hand. Keep hold until it swims away by itself.

Top: *A carp rug – a soft 'fish mattress' is used to lay the fish on when it is measured, the hook is removed, and while photographing.*

Bottom: *A big fish is held low over the carp rug to avoid injury if the fisherman should drop it.*

Top: *Small single hooks are best loosened with a disgorger.*

Bottom: *Hold the fish in the water and, if it seems exhausted, move it back and forth so that fresh water flows in through its mouth and over the gills. Do not let go until the fish swims away under its own power.*

Float angling – match angling

Match angling might appear complicated, but the principles are simple. With these in your baggage, you have a solid basis for varied fishing under widely different conditions and for numerous species – roach at the quay, bream at 40 m (130 ft) from land, spring perch in the deep holes of streams, grayling in the fast stretches of rivers, or tench at the reed edge on a balmy summer morning.

The float has an obvious function. It should succeed as rapidly as possible in presenting the bait where a fish is, to get a bite – and show the bite clearly. The tackle must also operate so that you are continuously able to keep the line stretched between the rod and float. Good line control is essential for hooking the fish before it lets go of the bait.

Flowing water

Stick float. A classic technique for flowing waters is to fish with a stick float. This is a thin, sensitive, pen-shaped float for low sinking weight, with an upper fuselage made of balsa and an underbody of bamboo. It is attached with rubber rings at top and bot-

Match angling with loosefeeding near land is superb for a number of species.

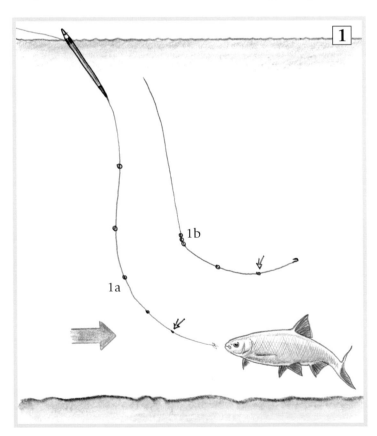

tom (like the Avon float below). By putting on an extra ring when tackling up, you avoid re-tying the tackle if one ring breaks.

The sinkers are spread along the line, with the heaviest one closest to the float and the lightest, called the signal shot, nearest the hook (Ill. 1a). Its placement and size determine how rapidly and clearly the take is seen. Cast out with a side-cast, where the line is 'feathered' – braking the cast with your finger against the reel – just before the tackle lands. Then the line stretches out and you see the bait taken 'on the drop' from the surface to the bottom.

The float should travel with the current downstream, the bait going before the tackle. The bail on the reel is open. Your index finger locks the line against the reel while the rod tip follows the float downstream. Line is released when the rod tip is moved back, with your finger off the reel. If the float dives, you lock the line again with your finger, raise the rod and hook the fish. Now and then the float is restrained and the bait rises, then falls through the water when the float is released again. The bite often comes when the bait is braked.

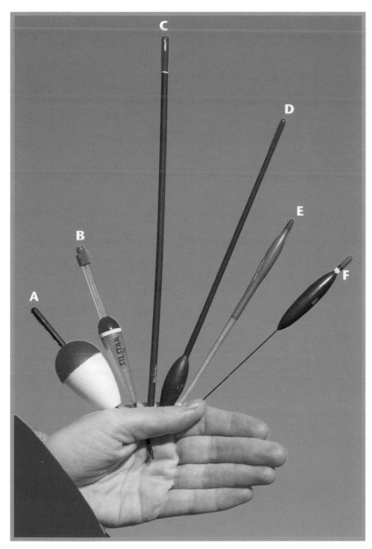

Different types of floats. From left: (A) Type previously used in Scandinavia for perch angling with baitfish – being large, chubby and insensitive, it is every-thing a modern float should not be. With such a float, the take cannot be seen before the fish has swallowed the bait and swum away. (B) An adequate float for perch fishing with a small baitfish. (C) Waggler for fishing in flowing waters, or still waters at close range. (D) Antenna float for medium to long distance in still waters. (E) Stick float and (F) Avon float for flowing waters

Roach is a classic match-angling species. Taken with a stick float in flowing waters, or an antenna float in still waters, combined with loosefeeding.

Combined with 'loosefeeding' (see Prebaiting) and light baits such as maggot, casters and corn grains, this method is very effec-tive for fish that can stand anywhere between the surface and bot-tom – roach, rudd, chub, ide and grayling. If the fish is standing closer to the bottom, a clump of shot is placed deeper, with the others spread below them. The bait will come down fast but its falling and rising movement can still be exploited (Ill. 1b).

A stick float is only useful in weak currents and one or two rod lengths out, at depths to about 10 feet (3 m), since it is easily pulled under. In strong currents, or if the fish will be standing farther out, an Avon float is more suitable.

Stick floats and Avon floats are usually fished with an overdepth – greater distance between the float and hook than the water depth, between 2–6 inches (5–15 cm). When the tackle is braked with the finger against the reel edge, the bait still wanders forward along the bottom. If the bite occurs only 'on the drop' and when you hold back strongly, the fish will stand higher and the distance between hook and float can be decreased.

Avon float

An Avon float is also tackled at top and bottom, but has a larger and more robust fuselage than the stick float (Ill. 2). It can bear more weight and take the bait deeper through stronger currents without being pulled under. Further, it can be held back and make the bait rise without the float rising out of the water – which would make it difficult to see the takes.

Since the Avon float is normally used for fish that stand deep, the shot is mostly placed in a clump about two-thirds of the way down from the float, the rest being spread out down to the hook. (The distance between shots should decrease all the way down to the hook, to prevent tangling by their catching on each other during the cast; this rule applies to all float tackle.)

The technique resembles that for stick-float fishing. You brake the tackle lightly and let the bait travel first. The Avon

Top left: Match angling is perfect for small baits such as a corn grain or a maggot.
Bottom left: Simple corn attracted one bream after the other.
Opposite Top: Even big carp can be taken with match angling.
Opposite Bottom: Fishing with an Avon float and waggler is ideal for chub.

Grayling are readily caught with a maggot and a stick or Avon float.

***Opposite:** Loosefeeding – casting or shooting out hooked baits – is an excellent method of prebaiting when fishing at close range, in both flowing and still waters.*

float is also excellent for fishing with large bread baits, which are very buoyant and need plenty of weight to be brought down to the right depth. It is used to catch chub, ide, large rudd and roach that stand deep. Moreover, it is perfect for 'long-trotting', where the float is allowed to travel far, up to 20–30 m (65-100 ft), for instance, when fishing for grayling or perch.

Waggler

In waggler fishing, the bait goes after the tackle (Ill. 3). This is fine when the fish stands at the bottom and wants bait that moves slowly. The float is fastened at the bottom and is fished with overdepth. The signal shot and the baited hook are dragged along the bottom by the current. A waggler float does not need to be held back to be effective, and it can be fished with upstream casts.

The sinker weights are placed in a clump 1.5–3 feet (0.5–1 m) over the bottom, with a few isolated shot between them and the signal shot. The stronger the current, the larger the sinker required to stay on the bottom, so the bigger the float. While it travels with the current, the float

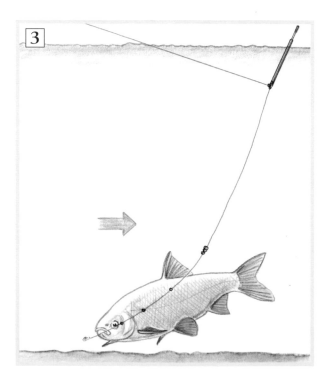

acquires a waggling gait as the sinker catches and lets go – hence the name of the method and the float.

Waggling is suitable for bream in every season, as well as for roach, perch and other species when the conditions make the fish stand at the bottom – cold weather or a hard current.

If the fish refuses to take a bait that moves at the pace of the tackle, you need to hold the float back. Try an Avon float with overdepth, which can be restrained without being pulled under. Release the tackle slowly downstream, little by little.

Still waters

At close range

Most still water float fishing is done with antenna floats – either with only one long antenna, such as a waggler float, or also with a long extra fuselage. They are fastened at the bottom through a small ring.

Fishing in middle to bottom waters

Up to seven or eight meters from land, a straight antenna float with a millimeter-thick extra top, or 'insert', is perfect. Buoyancy from a body is not needed; the float carries enough weight for casting and for bringing the bait to the desired fishing depth. With a few millimeters of insert over the water surface, the float is hypersensitive.

The shot are placed mostly around the float, as casting weight and so that it will rise directly, making the take visible. Just over halfway down, a 'semi-large' shot is placed. The next is the signal shot, 4–6 inches (10–15 cm) from the hook. This is a simple, sensitive tackle for virtually all fish that move between the bottom and a meter up. The halfway shot keeps the line stretched and quickly brings the bait to a depth where it slowly, attractively falls toward the bottom.

Depending on the takes, the sinkers are adjusted. If they delay minutes after the cast, the halfway shot is moved downward, as the fish wants the bait at the bottom. If they come lightning-fast, the fish takes the bait in the middle water, so you should move more weight up toward the float, or fish more shallowly.

Lift bite – fish at the bottom

When fishing at close range on the bottom, as for tench, a strong antenna float is needed It must carry a shot heavy enough to lie on the bottom and hold the bait in position. Sinkers that are sufficient as casting weight and to set up the float are placed around the float, but not more than enough to sink half the antenna. A sinker at the bottom should pull down until 1–2 cm (0.4-0.8 in) of the float sticks up. If the fish takes the bait and lifts the sinker, the float rises – a classic lift bite that thrills the heart of every lover of tench fishing. When the fish takes the bait sideways along the bottom, the float wanders away and is slowly pulled under.

Wind and surface current

When there is a wind or surface current, the line needs to be sunk between the float and rod tip Then an antenna float with more weight at the float is used. The extra sinker weight stabilizes it and gives extra casting length. Otherwise, the weighting is the same as for fishing in middle to bottom waters.

The cast is made some meters too long. With the rod tip under the surface, the line is wound in until the float reaches the fishing spot. Then the line is pulled under the surface and you can fish sensitively in spite of wind and current.

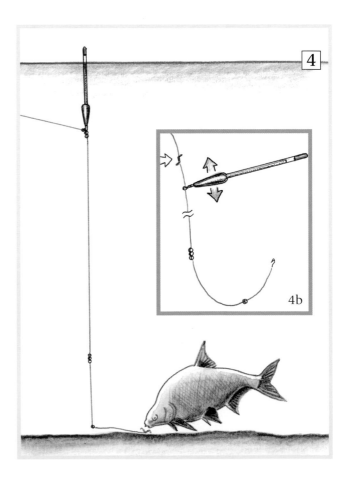

At long distance

For fishing at distances of 50–130 feet (15–40 m), large antenna floats are needed, with a body that takes considerable weighting (Ill. 4) – both to provide a long cast and to give good line control, since the effect of current and wind on the line increases with distance.

Most of the sinker lead is placed around the float, making it shoot like an arrow through the air. Farther down are some more robust sinkers to take the bait quickly down to the fish. How the sinkers sit there depends on the fish species. For fish such as roach, which can stand some way up in the water, the tackle resembles that for fishing in middle to bottom waters. For bottom-living fish such as bream, one or two pairs of large sinkers sit between the bulk and the signal shot. When the bait is to be presented on the bottom, often a big shot must lie on the bottom so that the float will not drift away due to current and wind. A sunken line works best.

There are antenna floats for long-distance fishing with a weighted body. They are excellent if you do not want much sinker on the line, as when the fish take bait in the middle water. In addition, they are good when a gliding float is needed, for fishing at greater depth than the rod length. The tackle then looks as described above, except that the float rests against the deeper shot and is stopped higher up on the line by a stop knot (Ill. 4b).

Weighted floats with a thin insert are of limited use. Small models can be employed for fishing at close range, when the fisherman wants a little shot on the line, but at long distance they do not work because the insert cannot be seen.

Sounding

A prerequisite for effective float angling is to sound the fishing depth. Sounding gives information on where slopes exist and terminate, whether there are deep holes, and what rubbish or vegetation may be out of sight on the bottom. Which part of the fishing place do roach or bream stand in? Which float should be chosen? How should it be adjusted if they do not bite, or stop biting?

A float angler sounds the place most easily by putting an extra weight on the hook and casting around in the area, so as to set the float properly. Special sounding sinkers are available, but at short distances it is also possible to use a heavy sinker such as an SSG clamped around the hook.

Close-range fishing with a light antenna float works very well for carp.

Bottom angling

Originally, bottom angling was an alternative when float angling did not work – for fishing at a great distance or depth, in strong currents or by dark. It has since grown into a very exciting technique of its own. In many cases, it is a better choice than float angling, not least for bottom species such as eel, tench, bream and carp. But it also helps in hunting bigger fish, which are often found on the bottom and may need to be caught under special conditions, as in the darkest hours of night.

Gliding bottom angling

In spite of its simplicity, the gliding technique of bottom angling is very effective for numerous species. Its ordinary variant can use standard spinning equipment, although a slightly longer rod of three meters (9 ft) or more is often best.

Gliding tackle for bottom angling is most easily made by threading the line through a pear sinker's swivel, knotting the hook on the line end, and stopping the sinker about 20 inches

Below and right: A good deal of bottom angling for large fish such as carp, eel, and tench is done with the rod in the holder, an electronic bite alarm and a monkey-climber, since there may be a long wait.

With a light stave at the top of the quivertip, it works perfectly after darkness falls.

(50 cm) up with a clamped lead shot. This works at close range with light sinkers of 15–25 grams (0.5-0.9 oz), but if the fishing is to be done with bigger sinkers or at greater distances, the lead shot may slide on the line and damage it at the cast.

Nylon leader. Instead, tie a leader of nylon with a hook and a swivel to the main line, after threading the line through the sinker's swivel. A plastic bead between the sinker swivel and the leader protects the knot. This is a simple and good tackle for fishing with large baits such as worms or some corn grains – for eel, tench, perch, bream and other species.

If you do not want to use an electronic bite alarm when fishing with gliding bottom angle, fold a piece of aluminum foil over the line between the first and second rod rings. The foil will rise at the take and fly off at the strike, without risking any tangle.

Soft leader. A variant of gliding tackle, developed for carp fishing with soft leader material and boilies (boiled paste balls

– see the chapter on baits), has the sinker attached to a plastic tube that the line is threaded through. A soft leader is used for tackle-shy fish, and the tube prevents the leader from tangling in the cast. The tube is longer than the leader to keep the hook from catching. The knot is protected by a plastic bead.

For all boilie fishing, a hair rig is outstanding, since the hook gets exposed and fastens better. An advantage with soft leader material is that it can be used to tie the hair rig – a line stump at the hook that the bait is threaded upon. This tackle also works well for tench. An adequate leader length is 16 inches (40 cm) for carp and 10 inches (25 cm) for tench. There are plenty of soft leader materials. My usual choices are 'Merlin' for carp and 'Silkworm' for tench, of the English brand Kryston. Soft leader materials are sensitive to wearing by stones and so forth, but Merlin has always endured, in contrast to other similar materials. Silkworm of 12 lbs (5.4 kg) strength, which is very thin and supple, is perfect for tench

Fishing with a swimfeeder is excellent for serving the prebait right at the hook bait, when bottom angling for a number of species.

***Top:** Bottom angling with boilies is extremely effective for tench.*
***Bottom:** Bream are a classic species in bottom angling with a swingtip or quivertip.*

The sinker can be exchanged for a swimfeeder to obtain a tackle for serving prebait on the bottom near the bait. This works best with a short hook leader, so that the hook bait and the prebait will not land too far from each other.

With heavier sinkers for fishing at great distance, or a swimfeeder heavy with prebait, the sinker leader may glide on the line during the cast. The solution is simple – a reversed paternoster. The sinker or swimfeeder is tied to the main line, and the hook leader is tied to it 8–12 inches (20–30 cm) farther up (This makes it easy to change to a thinner hook leader, as is sometimes necessary if the fish are cautious, without the entire tackle becoming too weak. For example, the main line can be 0.18 mm (0.007 In) and the leader 0.14 mm (0.005 In).

Sinker weights

The same principle holds for the sinker weight in bottom angling as in float angling: as light as possible, without causing a risk that the casts are too short or that the bait does not reach the bottom at the right place due to current. In flowing waters, when fishing for chub, rudd, roach and the like, the sinker's weight is particularly critical, and you may need to test several sizes before finding the perfect sinker.

The ideal is a sinker that barely manages to hold the bottom without being pulled by the current. The outward cast is made somewhat upstream, the bail is closed and, when the

Top: When the water is really cold, bottom angling is often superior to float angling, as the fish want a bait that lies still on the bottom.

Bottom: For eel, the gliding method of bottom angling is simplest and best.

A golden carp is returned after having plucked a boilie on a helicopter rig.

sinker reaches the bottom, it should preferably bounce a few times before it stops some way downstream of the fisherman. The current's force on the line makes the quivertip tense up in an arc. At the take, the sinker lightens and follows the fish downstream, giving it great difficulty in getting free of the hook. This is a kind of bolt effect, very effective for bites that can otherwise be hard to hook on.

In ordinary bolt-rig fishing, on the other hand, the sinker must not be too light, since the technique assumes that the fish will partly hook itself. With too light a sinker, there is a risk that the fish only feels the hook without letting it dig in. The weight should not be under 45 g (1.5 Oz) for carp, or 25 g (0.9 Oz) for tench.

Sounding

Simple sounding to find the right fishing depth, vegetation and so on, can be done with the help of the sinker. It does not give as good a picture of the fishing depth as sounding with a float, but is sufficient in most cases, and nothing else is possible when the fishing occurs far out.

Cast out and check the time until the sinker reaches the bottom. Bring the rod in, and feel how the sinker moves. If it slides, the bottom is probably a clean one such as clay. If it moves heavily but evenly, the bottom is soft and the sinker is plodding down in. If it catches and comes loose, the bottom may be very soft or have vegetation that brakes the sinker. Slight scraping means sand or gravel, while sharp bumps indicate stones.

Look for unusual places, where the fish stand. Clean sections amid dense vegetation are hot spots, and vice versa. If there is much soft bottom, areas with sand are perfect, and vice versa. The prebaiting should be concentrated there and the bait left lying.

The long rod

Top knot angling, with a line tied to the rod tip, gives perfect presentation of the bait. The fisherman can guide the tackle with centimeter-precision, let it wander a short distance with the current, hold back and let go again a little, thus almost 'vacuum-cleaning' the area of fish. This technique is preferred in competition fishing, unless the distance is too great or the fish that may bite are so big that they can tear off the tackle if the fisherman is unable to let out line.

Float tackle

This tackle is light, since no special casting weight is needed: the tackle is lifted out and the float need only carry the weight required to get the bait down to the right depth. Floats for still water are very slender, have low buoyancy, and can bear weights of less than a gram. Floats for flowing water are more compact and buoyant, as additional weight is necessary for the bait to reach a correct depth and maintain it, without the float rising in the water when held back and making the fish's take hard to see.

   Middle and lower water layers. Tackle for roach, and other fish from the middle waters to the bottom, has a concentrated weight – an elongated 'Olivetti' sinker, somewhat down on

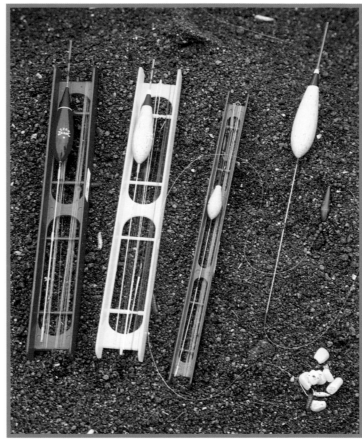

Since top knot tackle is so sensitive, the fisherman ties it at home where he/she has full control over how much weight is put on. Prepared tackles are stored in the attic and marked with weight, how the sinkers are placed, etc., so that one can change within seconds to the perfect tackle. The stronger the current, the lower the float's buoyancy sits. The floats shown here are for slowly flowing or still waters.

A long 'take-apart' rod gives the fishing great precision. When the fish are biting well, this approach is faster than both match angling and bottom angling, which makes it preferable for competition fishing.

← *Fishing with a long rod calls for a full-length line, enabling the fish to be lifted directly in. No time is wasted with this technique.*

→ *Take-apart means that the fishing can be done with the rod length that is best for the occasion. The line between the rod tip and the float is less than a meter. When fishing farther out than the fishing depth, you can pull in the rod until the position is suitable to take the rod apart and lift in the fish – or draw it over the landing net, if too big for the tackle to lift.*

the line – and below this a series of small shot, spread out in a similar way as for a stick float. The larger sinker quickly brings the tackle to the depth where the fish are, and the smaller weights keep the line stretched to the hook, which makes the tackle very sensitive to takes 'on the drop'.

At the bottom. Tackle for bream and other bottom fish have an Olivetti sinker placed closer to the hook. Below it are only one or two shot, which normally lie on the bottom. This allows the bait to lie still on the bottom until the fisherman, with a small movement of the rod, pulls it a short distance and waits again .

Flowing water. The difference in flowing waters is basically just that you need larger weights and that the Olivetti sinker is often closer to the hook. The fish usually stand deeper, and more weight is needed to get the bait rapidly down through the current, as well as to restrain the tackle.

Take-apart

With a take-apart rod, the fishing is exact to the millimeter. The line between the rod tip and the float is shorter than a meter, and the slightest movement with the rod is transferred to the tackle. A little line over the water surface makes it easier to control the tackle if the wind is strong. This technique is used primarily in competition fishing, and has been developed for the most hard-fished waters, with fish that are small or shy of tackle. Here you need lines, sinkers and floats that are as thin and light as possible in order to get any bites at all.

The combination of thin line – leader material down to 0.06 mm (0.002 in) is used – and a short line means that the tackle can easily break off. Therefore, a 'shock absorber' is often included: a rubber band about a meter long, placed in the top part of the rod, where it softens the fish's lunges and jerks. With this technique, surprisingly big fish can be caught even on very thin lines. Occasionally, the rubber is stretched several meters when a sizable fish pulls away.

Prebaiting– the foundation for success

Prebaiting brings more bites by bigger fish. It has made catchable and sought-after sportfish out of species that were regarded as too wild forty years ago.

Although prebaiting is the basis of modern angling, it does not automatically yield fish. Like other fishermen, the angler must choose the place where the chances are greatest that fish will exist or pass by, before he prebaits – apart from competition fishermen who have to make the best of their position and, nonetheless, find their chief weapon in prebaiting.

The fish's natural behavior is the key. How do wind and current influence it? Where in a lake does a certain species live, at what depth, on which bottom?

Sounding

The specimen fisherman has a good deal to learn from competition fishermen about sounding. They investigate their place in detail. Where do slopes exist and flatten out? Are there deep holes, invisible vegetation, or rubbish on the bottom? Then they decide how and where to fish and prebait.

Sounding also gives other kinds of information. Where are different species located at the fishing place? Which tackle works best? How should it be adjusted if the fish do not bite, or stop biting? (See the technical sections on sounding.) Prebaiting before sounding is like fishing blindly.

Loosefeeding

To cast a few baits out at a time, or shoot them out with a sling, is called loosefeeding. It is done regularly in order to attract and captivate the fish, but not so often – or with so many baits – that the fish become satisfied.

When to loosefeed. Loosefeeding is perfect for bottom angling and float angling at a short distance, in both still and flowing waters. The latter require the fisherman to judge where the current takes the free food. The hook bait should go the same way, at the same depth. Baits such as maggots and casters (the pupae of maggots) can drift for a long distance, and must be cast upstream of the fishing spot. Heavier baits such as corn sink quickly and are cast just over the float. Loosefeeding is often better than accompanying the hook bait with prebait bread, which satisfies the fish more – especially in winter, when it is easy to prebait too much.

Loosefeeding involves casting the baits or shooting them out with a slingshot. In still waters, the prebaiting can be done exactly over the fishing spot; when float angling, the float can be aimed at. In flowing waters, the fisherman must estimate how far the stream takes the baits before they reach the right fishing depth – where the hook will be.

Specimen anglers get valuable lessons from competition fishermen, who investigate the spot thoroughly before prebaiting. One prebait may be laid just outside reeds, for fish that cruise along the inner edge, and another pre-bait farther out at an interesting structure such as the next edge.

Tactics. The arrangement of float and sinker may need adjustment during the fishing. Frequently the fish stand deep at first, when the float must be set so that the bait is directly on or over the bottom. Food cast out makes the fish rise, and ever more bites can come higher up in the water. Shallower fishing is then needed, with the lead shot more dispersed so that the tackle catches in free water.

Baits may still fall past the fish and be left lying. These can attract larger fish that calmly pick up food from the bottom. Set the float deeper again after a while and make the day's biggest catch.

Bread prebaiting

Bread prebait is brown dried bread – lightly 'toasted' and white – which is untreated, mixed with additives to give taste or special qualities. These may be sticky ingredients that make

Rudd is a species that responds well to loosefeeding, for example with corn or maggots.

For carp, loosefeeding with corn near land is an excellent method.

Left: When fishing near the surface with bread, for example, one also loose-feeds the attractor baits around the hook bait with a slingshot.
Above: Bread prebait is a 'transport medium' for the attractor baits, and draws fish with a good scent and taste. Before shooting out a load, it is good to squeeze all the balls, making them easier to shoot with precision.

the bread hold together, or others that make it crack quickly. This depends, for example, on whether the fisherman wants the prebait to break up on the surface or on the bottom. Ready mixes can be bought.

The prebait has two functions. First, it carries baits such as maggots, worm, corn and other morsels to a fishing place far out, or through strong current. And secondly, it attracts the fish with its scent and taste. The fact that the prebait is eaten should be kept in mind so as not to prebait excessively.

Mixing. Bread prebait is moistened at intervals. The dry bread is put in a bowl, water is poured in, and the blend is stirred until the prebait holds together, without feeling sticky when you take a handful and squeeze. Then it is left standing for half an hour to absorb, before mixing in more water – with caution, since too much can easily be added.

Additives for taste and scent are applied before the wetting if they are in powder form, or with the water if they are in liquid form.

Once the prebait is adequately wet, the bait is mixed in. Maggots are added only when they are about to go out, because lying in wet prebait can liquefy them.

Close range – at the bottom. When fishing at close range for large bottom fish, bread prebait is ideal for getting the bait to the bottom. The bread sneaks the prebait past small fish.

But it is important for the ball to hold together until it reaches the bottom. The same is true of fishing in strong currents. If the prebait breaks up too soon, fish are lured away from the place, as they follow the cloud of prebait downstream. To make prebait that holds well, 20–40 percent of white bread can be mixed with the brown.

Close range – free water. The opposite is done when fishing in free water, as for roach in the summer, or by float angling in flowing waters for chub and rudd. They want the bait in the middle water and are attracted by a cloud of prebait. Pure brown bread, lightly squeezed, works perfectly.

Long range. Prebaiting at a greater distance for bottom species, such as bream, is more difficult. The prebait has to hold in order to be cast or slung out. The bait must get to the bottom quickly so as not to draw smaller fish. But prebait balls that crash down like cannonballs can kill the fishing.

If a few small fish are about, the best prebait balls are those that can take being slung out, but crack on the surface. Shoot them out with a low trajectory, so that they crack with a low 'puff'. Mix in 15–20 percent of white bread, and be very careful with the wetting. It is a good idea to sieve the prebait after wetting. If there are many small fish, abundant prebaiting is done at the outset with prebait that holds, and then none as long as the fish are biting well.

Left: Bread prebait is shot out with a slingshot.
Below: Tench is among the many species that are attracted by a blend of bread prebait and hook baits.

Frequency. A golden rule in all prebaiting is to do a little and do it often. Start with a couple of prebait balls and follow with a smaller ball every ten minutes. If the fish bite immediately, increase the amount. In summertime, a little can be thrown out for every bite. It requires both simultaneous action and precision to hook and play fish while also throwing food to the right place.

Flingbread. Dry bits of bread in the prebait are fatally effective for numerous species, when fishing with bread as a bait. This includes chub and rudd during summer longtrotting or swimfeeder fishing in autumn, winter and spring – as well as tench, carp and bream, caught by the lift method or by bottom angling with a swingtip.

The dry bread floats with the current, or climbs slowly toward the surface in still waters, and helps to create a real explosion of the prebait from a swimfeeder.

Swimfeeders

With a swimfeeder, prebaiting is done right at the hook bait. There are special models for maggots, closed at the ends but having holes for the larvae to crawl out through. Swimfeeders for prebait bread are open at the ends.

Winter technique. Since the prebaiting is exact, there is scant risk of overdoing it. This makes a swimfeeder good for fishing in the cold season, as when going after chub, barbel, rudd and roach. By using a swimfeeder only during the first three or four casts, then exchanging it for a sinker, the risk of excessive prebaiting is further reduced.

Distance fishing. A swimfeeder is superb at greater distances, where prebait can be hard to throw out exactly. It is also a good tactic when there are big fish at the bottom under schools of small fish.

In distance fishing with a swimfeeder, one begins by casting often during the first 10–15 minutes. The tackle should lie for only half a minute or so at a time. Once this basis is established, the tackle can lie longer and the bites determine the amounts of prebait. Many bites lead to frequent casts and much prebait, and vice versa. The prebaiting is adapted to the quantity of fish at the spot.

As the prebaiting should draw the fish to the hook bait, the casts must be exact. Aim at something on the other side of the lake or stream, and cast equally far each time. This is especially hard at great distances. Therefore, cast about a meter farther out than the fishing spot and set a wide rubber band over the spool,

A swimfeeder is superb for placing the prebait precisely at the hook bait, for prebaiting little during the colder seasons, for getting prebait through schools of small fish to bigger fish on the bottom, and for prebaiting at great distances.

before you start to prebait. With prebait in the feeder, cast so that the spool is stopped by the rubber band. When the tackle has landed, wind in a few turns and every cast will be right.

Prebait bread for a swimfeeder should be less wet than when it is thrown out. Then it explodes from the feeder when the bread absorbs water.

Opposite:
Top: Bream is a classic 'swimfeeder species'.
Bottom: During the cold season, swimfeeder fishing is one of the best methods for chub, since it spreads small portions of attractive worms exactly at the hook bait with little risk of excessive prebaiting.

Tench are among the species, including carp, which respond best to boilie prebaiting.

Prebaiting with boilies

Boilies are particularly good when prebaiting for tench, since they largely sort out undesired fish. The fish must also learn to eat then, as they are not natural like worms and maggots. Once boilies are eaten, they are amazingly effective and the fish become almost 'addicted'. The required time varies between waters. In some cases they are taken immediately; in others, it may take weeks. In certain waters they work ever better with each season.

Method. The most common tool for boilie prebaiting is with a slingshot, but a casting tube is often better if the baits are to go really far out.

Quantity. The choice of place is very important, as boilie prebaiting takes time and work. One must have an idea of how many fish may come to the spot. In waters with fish such as roach and bream, however, it is difficult to prebait too much because they eat up the boilie remains, unless carp and tench have done so after a couple of days.

If a tour is to continue for a week or two, it is good to begin with a small quantity every few days during the first week, and to prebait more on a daily basis during the second week.

Pattern. Spread out the prebait at first, so that the fish learn to recognize the bait. Cover their routes around the fishing place. Then bring the prebaiting inward and, finally, do it only where the hook baits are to lie.

Opposite:
Top left and bottom left: A casting tube is an alternative to a slingshot for getting boilies far out. It can easily be made from a plastic tube of suitable diameter. It is also good for rapidly strewing large amounts of particle bait such as corn near land.
Right: Water-soluble PVA string is a fine method of pinpoint prebaiting with boilies. It is good in cold water or where much fishing has taken place earlier with abundant boilies.

When fishing, prebait just around the hook bait. Prebait more in the summer and less in cold water, when five or six baits can be enough.

PVA. To avoid excessive prebaiting when fishing in autumn, the prebaiting can make use of a PVA string, which dissolves in water after a few minutes – if it works as it should. Try it ashore, with some baits on a stump of string.
Thread 4 to 6 baits on a piece of PVA string and tie it directly to the hook. After the cast, the string dissolves and the prebait lies some centimeters from the hook bait.

There are also small bags, and net-tubes of PVA that can be cut to a suitable bag length. They are filled with boilies, corn and so on, tied to the tackle and cast out. Thus one can prebait a whole portion precisely at the hook bait.

Combination prebaiting

Prebaiting that blends boilies and particle baits such as corn is effective for species such as carp and tench. The small baits attract and engage the fish without satisfying them, and the fish find good morsels just like the fisherman's hook bait. This tactic is common in large lakes of Southern Europe with plenty of fish, where masses of food are needed to keep the fish at the place, and the prebaiting is often done easily from a boat.

If the fisherman has no boat, a 'spod' can be used. This is a swimfeeder filled with a few deciliters of small bait. It is cast out to the fishing spot with another rod, emptied and wound in again for a new load.

Prebaiting

With prebaiting one tries to gain several advantages:
- Luring the fish to start eating at the spot. Separate baits are cast into the water and make bite-shy fish curious.
- Attracting more fish to the spot.
- Persuading the fish to eat a special bait.
- Reducing the fish's suspicions. If they swim up every time they eat corn, they will stop eating corn. If they eat 100 grains before being hooked, the corn will work longer.

Far left: *Bags of PVA can be used to lay small portions of boilies and particle bait for tasting near the hook bait.*

Above : *A 'spod' is a little swimfeeder that is loaded with small bait and cast out with an extra rod. This is an excellent way of prebaiting at a distance with particle bait.*

Bottom: *In Southern Europe, prebaiting is done with huge quantities of baits in many waters, since the water temperature is high and the fish are plentiful and gluttonous. Either a boat or a 'spod' is used.*

Baits for angling

All the baits used in angling are of natural origin. And only the angler's imagination sets the limits: everything from worms, larvae and seeds, to pastes that the angler concocts in the kitchen with flour and other ingredients can be included. Here a choice of baits is presented, with tips on tackle and a deep dive into the manufacture of angling's 'high-tech' bait – the boilie. Throughout, the basic principle is that the hook size is selected according to the bait's size.

Right: Worms, or combination, worm/caster or worm/corn are one of the best baits for bream.

1 Boilies are the super-bait for tench and carp. The bait sits on a hair rig (see the chapter on carp), locked against the little stop. The hook must be un-angled and strong enough for carp, in sizes 2–6 for baits of 16–20 mm (0.6-0.8 in). Here is the Fox Specialist Carp, series 2, size 2. Tench require a thinner hook of size 8–10 for baits of 10–14 mm (0.4-0.5 in). This is the Drennan Starpoint, size 10. The thin silicon piece behind the bait fixes it in the right position on the hook.

2 Corn is a universal bait for carpfish. And no bait is simpler to find than by buying a can of corn. Hooks of size 10 for several corn grains and size 14 for a single one. Use a slightly thicker hook for tench and chub, such as the Drennan Super Specialist. For bream, roach and rudd, you need a thinner hook, like the Kamazan B530.

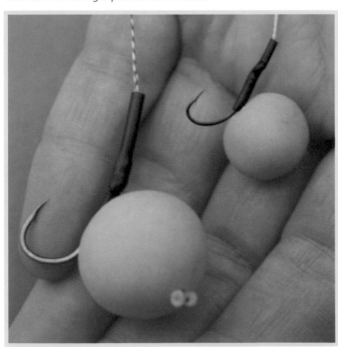

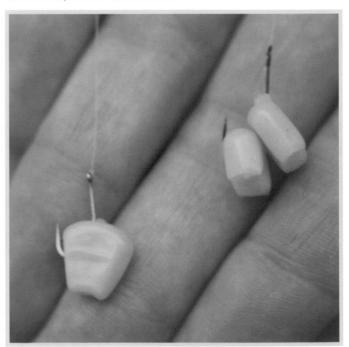

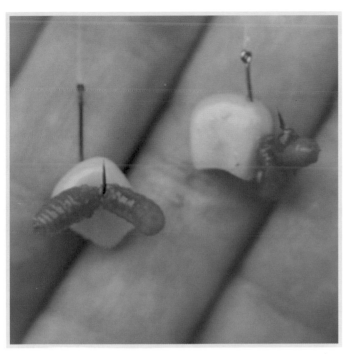

3 Corn and maggots are among the commonest and best combination baits. Here on a thinner hook, Kamazan B530 for bream, roach and rudd, or a thicker hook such as Drennan Super Specialist for tench, chub and barbel. Size 10.

4 Earthworms are some of the most familiar and effective baits for big fish. A hook of size 2–4 is adequate for eel. Tench, chub, perch and carp require size 4–6. They stay fresh longer if kept cool in moistened newspaper.

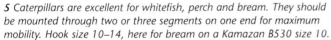

5 Caterpillars are excellent for whitefish, perch and bream. They should be mounted through two or three segments on one end for maximum mobility. Hook size 10–14, here for bream on a Kamazan B530 size 10.

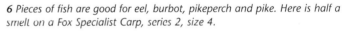

6 Pieces of fish are good for eel, burbot, pikeperch and pike. Here is half a smelt on a Fox Specialist Carp, series 2, size 4.

7 Shrimp is a lethal bait for eel, chub and tench, among other species. For eel, it should sit as shown here. The hook is a Fox Specialist Carp, series 2, size 4.

8 White bread does well for all carpfish. The hook must have a wide gap so that the bait stays on. It is superb for chub and rudd in float or bottom angling, and as floating bait. Here a piece of crust is on a Drennan Wide Gape Specialist, size 6, in a morsel adequate for chub.

9 The inner crumb from white bread, which should be fresh, is good for all carpfish and is used widely for roach, rudd and chub. A strip is folded round the hook – push it over the hook eye. It hangs fluffy around the hook without hindering the hooking. Small pieces loosen and drift attractively with the current.

10 Bread paste is another classic carp-fishing bait. Wide-gap hook, size 4–10. White bread is wetted and kneaded into a non-sticky paste. Other tit-bits, such as blue cheese for chub, can be kneaded into the paste for extra appeal. The hook must have a broad gap, as does the Drennan Wide Gape Specialist, here in size 6.

11 *Cheese is a time honored chub bait. The hook is a broad-gap model such as Drennan Wide Gape Specialist, here in size 6. A piece of cheese is kneaded until soft and shaped into a ball. It hardens when dipped in water, giving good protection against attacks by small fish, or a piece can be cut directly from the cheese and attached to the hook as it is.*

12 *Maggots, or fly larvae, are the primary bait for roach and rudd when fishing with loosefeeding. Single ones on hook 18, or bunches for bigger fish such as bream, like three shown here on size 10 (Kamazan B 530).*

13 *Casters, or pupated maggots, are regarded in England as especially good for large roach. They also do well for bream. Must be fished on a thin hook such as this Kamazan B 530, size 18.*

14 *Worms and casters are fine for most whitefish, and outstanding for larger bream. With a caster, the worm sits better during long casts. Casters require a thin hook such as the Kamazan B 530, here in size 10.*

Boilies

Ready-made boiliers can be purchased, but it is much more fun to fish with your own. They often catch more fish, too, and are cheaper. In addition, they can be tailor-made for special conditions. This is not even hard. Ingredients can be found in ordinary shops or sportfishing stores.

Raw materials and equipment

Raw materials

- **Dry mix:** either ready-mixed or home-mixed (see recipe at the end). The flour it contains determines the boilie's nutrient content, hardness and density.
- **Eggs** (six, and about 1 lbs of dry mix, give around 2 lbs of baits).

Ingredients and equipment for making paste. Ready-blended dry mix, flavorings, oil, large bowl to blend in, whip, wooden ladle, and table knife to scrape the ladle with.

Blend the flavorings, oil, powder additives such as sweetener and nutrient supplements, and water. Whip thoroughly.

- **Flavoring and aromatic substances.** They attract the fish, give the bait a good taste, and enable the fisherman to create a bait with unique taste and scent.
- **Sweetener.** Sweets are adored by carp and make other tastes "richer". Can be anything from concentrated sweeteners to sugar.
- **Nutritious supplements.** Amino acids, vitamins and minerals.
- **Oil.** Gives the bait more fat content and makes it easier to roll.
- **Water.** Helps distribute the flavorings and improves the rolling.

Pour in about 3 cups of dry mix and blend well. Work in more and more powder.

Place the ready paste in a plastic bag. Let it "rest" for 10-30 minutes.

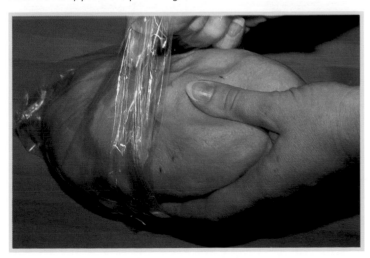

Equipment

- **Rollboard.** A tray with parallel half-tubes and matching lid. Lengths of the dough, as wide as the tubes, are laid across the board and the lid put on. Press down, and the lengths are divided and shaped into round balls when the lid is moved back and forth. Then it is swept forward to roll them off the tray. Such a board saves time and is available for baits from 8 to 28 mm (0.3-1 in) thick, as well as in different widths for 8-10 to 20-30 baits per dough length.
- **Food syringe.** Load it with half a mix per session. Different nozzles are used to vary the diameter of the dough length pressed out, so that it fits the rollboard. This tool is handy when many mixes are made at once. If a syringe is used, the mix should be softer than when hand-rolling, so that it can be pressed through. A sticky mix can be helped through with a little flour on the nozzle.
- **Cutting-board,** to roll and slice the dough lengths on.
- **Sharp knife,** for cutting the dough to the right length.
- **Baking-plate,** to lay the balls on while waiting for boiling. Flour it to prevent the baits from sticking.
- **Large pot.**
- **Colander,** for pouring out baits made from boiled paste.
- **Towel,** to lay out the baits until they dry.
- **Plastic bags** for freezing.
- **Pen** for marking the bags (mix, taste, day).

Rolling equipment. At left: large board and syringe (with nozzles for different bait sizes). At right: smaller board for hand-rolled lengths of dough, cutting-board to roll lengths on, and a sharp knife to cut the lengths with. Roll a whole mix and lay the balls on a floured baking-plate to await boiling.

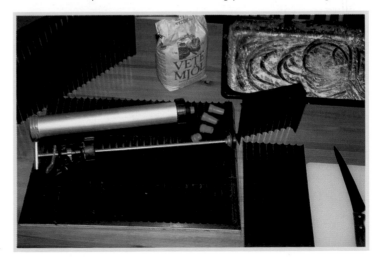

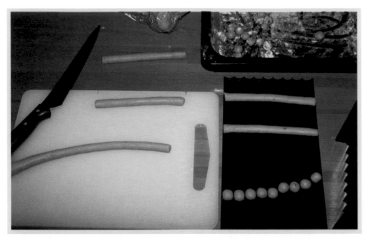

Left: Lengths of dough are rolled and cut; two are laid across the board. The lid is put on, pressed, moved back and forth, then out over the plate at last with the ready balls.

Below: With the syringe, two or three lengths are pressed out across the board, the lid goes on, and after a few swipes the balls are finished.

Bottom left: After rolling a mix, it is tipped into a large pot of water being heated. Stir carefully so that they do not stick. In 2–3 minutes the baits are done, even if the water has not reached boiling point.

Bottom right: From the pot, the baits are poured into a colander.

Flow plan for smooth work

1. Dry-mix ingredients to make 5-10 mixes each time, which saves effort. Between the rollings, keep the mix in a bucket with tight-fitting lid.
2. Blend the wet phase: 6 eggs, flavorings, water and cooking oil. Add sweetener and nutrient/vitamin supplement. Whip.
3. Pour in about 3 cups of dry mix and blend well. Using all the powder at once makes it hard to mix, spreads the ingre-

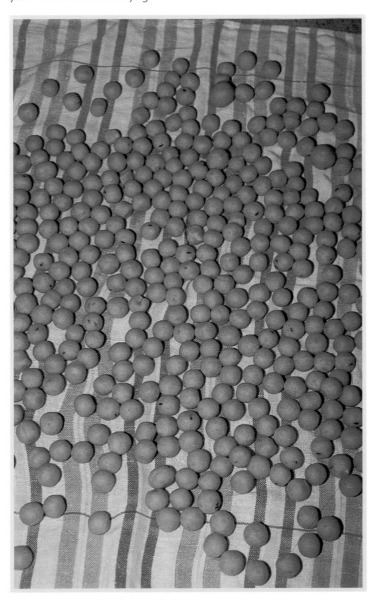

From the colander, tip the baits onto a towel. Roll them occasionally with your hand for all-round drying.

dients unevenly and toughens the paste. Then add more powder and work it in until the paste is semi-soft without sticking. Let the paste "rest" in a plastic bag for 10-30 minutes. The powder absorbs the fluid well, the paste stiffens and it becomes easier to roll. If it is too soft after resting, knead in more mix.

4. Roll lengths of suitable diameter on the rollboard or press them out with a syringe. Cut in lengths that fit the board's width, or press them out across the board. Make about ten lengths before rolling. Dry lengths roll badly. The number that can be made between rollings depends on how fast the paste dries, which varies with different mixes. The balls are laid on a floured baking-plate until the whole mix has been rolled.
5. Boil. Fill a large pot halfway with water and heat it. Pour in all the mix at once, and stir at regular intervals. It does not matter if the water stops boiling, as less of the flavoring and aromatics will then disappear. Pour out in a colander after a suitable time (depending on the mix and desired hardness, 2-3 minutes are usually enough) and quickly onto a towel for drying.
6. Dry thoroughly, for at least 1-2 and ideally 10-12 hours; longer time gives harder baits. Roll the baits around with your palm now and then, to dry them all over, before being packed in plastic bags and frozen. Boilies last for at least a year when frozen. One mix per half hour is about what one person can expect to manage without a syringe.

Drying - an alternative to freezing

Boilies take up much freezing volume, but an alternative is drying - mankind's oldest method of conservation.

1. Mix and boil as usual.
2. Dry the baits on a towel for 1-2 days, rolling them at times with your hand.
3. Place the baits in women's nylon stockings (it is worth buying a dozen pairs at a lingerie sale). A knee-length stocking holds about one and a half mixes.
4. Hang the stockings in a drying cupboard and run it for 1-2 hours at moderate power (too high a temperature cracks the baits). Lift the stockings a few times so that the baits shift and air reaches everywhere). At room temperature it takes longer, about a week.
5. Store the baits in a dry airy place, for instance hanging in the stockings, until they are used.

If the baits are to be preserved by drying, fill a ladies' stocking with them after 1–2 days of drying on a towel. The stockings are then hung in a dry place.

The baits become very hard, so a bag of frozen hook baits is needed when fishing. Dried baits can be soaked in a water mixture with a little taste/scent substance to acquire extra fragrance. Thus, 12-24 hours before they are to be used, pour them into a large plastic bag (1 mix), add diluted flavoring (1 part to 10-15 of water), blow up the bag, close it and shake. Keep shaking until all the liquid is absorbed. Dried baits have a lifetime of several years. Once in the water, they still emit an aroma and are loved by carp in spite of their hardness!

Recipes

HNV (High Nutritional Value)
Mix with a balanced nutrient content (protein, fat, carbohydrates), which becomes ever better as the fish learn how beneficial it is. With this mix, and accompanied by two friends, I took over 50 carp in a Swedish lake of 600 hectares with hardly a hundred carp in it, during 14 days of fishing. Two thirds of what other fishermen caught in the lake all season!

Dry phase: 1/4 cup milk albumin, 3/4 cup casein, 1/4 cup calcium caseinate (milk proteins), 1 cup milk powder, 1 2/3 cups full-fat soy flour, 1/4 cup egg albumin (protein), 1/4 cup wheat gluten, 1/4 cup semolina, 1/4 cup wheat-bran, 1/4 cup sugar, 2 tsp vitamin supplement (for dogs, from a pet shop). Liquid phase: 6 eggs, 3 Tbsp cooking oil, 2 Tbsp water, flavoring andaromatic substances (we had two combinations: 2 tsp kiwi + 3 drops eucalyptus oil, and 2 tsp hazelnut + 1 tsp peanut oil).

Base mix

"Service-store mix". To be used directly, or blended with a cup or two of fish meal or bird food (from a fishery or pet shop). It gives simple variants that are very effective due to their inherently carp-attracting tastes and scents.

Dry phase: 1 1/4 cups milk powder, 1/2 cup soy isolate, 1 2/3 cups full-fat soy flour, 1 1/4 cups semolina. Liquid phase: 6 eggs, 2 Tbsp cooking oil, 1 Tbsp water, flavoring and aromatic substances.

Both of the above recipes can be supplemented with concentrated sweeteners and so forth. For baits with different qualities, vary the proportions between ingredients. Milk proteins, egg albumin and semolina give harder baits; casein and semolina make them heavier, while egg albumin, soy isolate and caseinates make them lighter.

Opposite.
Top: Worms, corn, bread, maggots, boilies...the list of good tench baits is long.
Bottom: Bread bits are a classic bait for chub.

Practical fishing

Carp   Cult fishing

From an obscure occupation of eccentrics, carp fishing has grown into a cult for people from all social classes. By now the dominant branch of modern angling, and of carp equipment and baits, it enjoys a turnover in the multi-millions. Many of the techniques that were originally developed for this 'queen of the river' are also increasingly used for numerous other species.

Size

The popularity of carp fishing has to do, of course, with the fact that the fish can become very big indeed. There are carp weighing over 40 kg (88 lb) in North America, perhaps over 50 kg (110 lb). Specimens over 35 kg (77 lb) have been landed in Southern Europe, and over 20 kg (44 lb) in Scandinavia. With their size goes raw strength, and whoever has hooked a wildly rushing carp of 10 (22 lb) or 15 kg (33 lb) understands the comparison to catching onto a fast-approaching freight train.

Hard to fool

But it also has to do with the difficulty of luring carp and the bad experiences they teach. A carp fisherman who wants to succeed in the long run must be thoughtful. Plan, lay up strategies, and have an idea of why he proceeds in a certain way to trick the next giant into making a mistake. At the risk of irritating some practitioners of spinning, I like to point out a difference: every spinning cast requires a second's thought – about where to cast – and the cast is fished for something like twenty seconds. Behind every carp-fishing cast lie many hours of preparation, and it can fish for twenty hours.

Curing the soul

Last, but not least important, is the contrast between laid-back immobility and explosive excitement. On the spot, after all preparations are made and the baits are cast at carefully selected locations, all you can do is wait. A wait that gives such calm and total relaxation that it is a form of cure for the soul. Like a spice, there is always the feeling that something can happen in a fraction of a second.

Choice of place

A key factor of success in fishing for carp is the choice of place.

Left: The charm of carp fishing includes the total relaxation a fisherman experiences while awaiting a bite, after the baits are cast out and the rods are in the holders.

A golden reward as a carp morning breaks.

The simplest and most general rule is that it is best to fish where the wind blows in, with the wind in your face.

Obviously, though, other factors play a role – and an ever more significant one as the fishing session becomes longer, or the campaign is extended at a given place with prebaiting. It is rather meaningless to begin three weeks of prebaiting in a southward-opening cove because the wind blows from that direction just then, but from other directions 95 percent of the time. Thus, for longer fishing, it is better to choose a place that lies right for the wind during the following days of fishing, or for most of the season if the effort continues for a month or more.

Structures

Carp mainly eat from the bottom and are attracted by bottom changes. Most of the food is there. Currents bring organic material, and a varied bottom provides space for all the small animals that live on it. The principle is about the same as the fact that dust does not collect in the middle of a flat floor, but in corners, around furniture, behind the TV and so on.

Such areas are called structures in fishing terminology. Examples are a reedy edge where a slope planes out, a shallow section of an even bottom, an area with hard bottom surrounded by soft bottom, and a pondweed belt surrounded by free water. Precipices, vegetation, and bottom contrasts can be found by casting about with a sinker, weighing 60–80 g (2.1-

Top: *A fish with a paddle of this size is understandably strong. Hooking a 10 kg (20 lb) carp can be compared with catching a hook on a passing train.*

Bottom: *Two-toned carp are a special variant, usually due to a nerve injury that has put the fish's color control out of order. It can also be seen in other carpfish such as bream and tench.*

Top: *Mountain carp are closest to wild carp, and big specimens are the carp fisherman's most coveted quarries.*

Bottom: *Carp include all possible variants of color. Such are the well-known kio carp, also an enjoyable pond and aquarium fish, as well as golden-hued 'common' carp.*

2.8 oz), and slowly pulling it in while feeling how it behaves (see the chapter on bottom angling).

One of the very best and most neglected structures is the shore zone – but more about that later.

Baits

Boilies

The leading baits for carp fishing are boilies. They sort out smaller fish that are undesirable in the context of carp. Hence it is perfect for the prebaiting campaigns that raise the chances of success.

An aspect to consider, especially when visiting waters with hard fishing pressure, is the benefit of boilies with high nutritional value. This theory was quite popular during the 1970s when boilies were a novelty, but today it tends to be forgotten. A nutritious bait, after prebaiting, will be preferred by the fish to a bait with low nutrient content.

Here a domestic devil has an advantage, since he possesses full control over what is in the bait. He can also tailor-make it in other ways and acquire a lead over other fishermen. For just as in all fishing, doing things differently pays off. The taste, size, color, and nutrient content should be varied.

Perfect taste

The desire to find the perfect bait is a key factor behind the development of boilie flavors. Fruity ones were used most at first, but now there are no limits to what is mixed in the search for unique taste and scent. Or how does octopus with whiskey sound? Personally, I prefer more natural variants, and have had greatest success with types such as raspberry, tutti-frutti, hazelnut and pistachio.

Particle baits

Preserved corn is the most universal particle bait, but there are plenty of others. Fodder corn, chickpeas, soybeans, kidney beans, tiger nuts, peanuts, and hemp are examples.

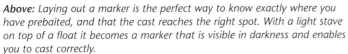

Above: Laying out a marker is the perfect way to know exactly where you have prebaited, and that the cast reaches the right spot. With a light stave on top of a float it becomes a marker that is visible in darkness and enables you to cast correctly.

Top right: The carp's sucking mouth and barbels are well suited to plucking bait from the bottom, and the entire area around its mouth is full of taste and scent receptors, giving it a fine sense of smell. Carp fishermen make use of this by flavoring their bait in all possible ways.

Right: With the boilie on a short hair right next to the hook, the fish is hooked perfectly in the corner of the mouth.

Canned corn is ready to use, but dry particle baits need to be prepared. They are placed in water for one or more days, and then boiled. This prevents them from injuring the fish. A fish that eats dry baits could even die when they swell in its stomach. When soaking, the baits can be given a personal touch by adding some flavoring. The duration of soaking and boiling, as well as how the baits take up tastes vary for different baits. The bigger and harder they are, the longer it can take. But a good main rule is to soak them for at least a day and night.

Top right: A waggler or antenna float, leaded overdeep, and a little corn are all that is needed for sneak fishing.

Bottom: Fishing in the magic margins offers close encounters.

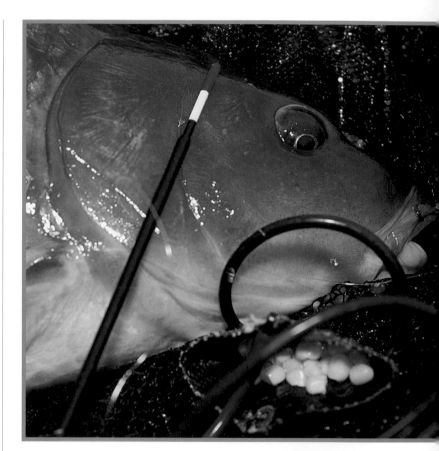

The 'hair rig'

For boilies and large particle baits to be effective, the hook must be exposed. Therefore a 'hair rig' is used: a stump of line with a ring at the end, tied to the hook in diverse lengths and variants, The bait is threaded with a boilie needle, similar to a knitting needle, and is prevented from falling off by a piece of a matchstick or a 'boilie stop'. The rig's name derives from the fact that its 'hair' was initially made by the 'inventor' from strands of his own hair.

Short hair

I use mostly short hair. To minimize the risk of the bait 'obscuring' the hook tip, a short piece of silicon tubing is placed on the leader .When the boilie has been threaded on, the tubing is pushed up over the hook eye against the boilie. The hook then lies alongside the bait, at a 90-degree angle. It catches efficiently, almost always in one of the carp's mouth corners, and sits securely – while easy to loosen without damaging the fish.

Hook

The best boilie hooks are chemically polished with a straight shaft, and have a wide gap and an inward-curved tip. They catch well with no risk of tearing up the fish's mouth. Sizes 2–6 prevail, the choice being adapted to the bait size.

Hook baits 'Pop-up'

As hook bait, ordinary boilies or particle bait can be used. Better, however, is a hook bait that distinguishes itself, so that the carp finds it faster than others. A common variant is a floating hook bait, or 'pop-up'. Normally it is weighted with a lead shot, so as to hover a few centimeters above the bottom. It is seen better and can more easily release attractive scents.

Boosted baits

Hook baits that are 'boosted' – dipped in a diluted mixture of flavorings, amino acids and the like – are deadly effective.

Since carp primarily use their superb sense of smell to find food, a bait that smells more than others will inevitably be taken first. Further versions of a 'plum in the pudding' are a larger hook bait, a different color, more on the rig, and so on.

Prebaiting

One cornerstone of the carp-fishing world is prebaiting. It teaches the fish to eat at a given place and is often necessary for making them pick 'unnatural' particle baits or boilies without suspicion.

Distance fishing

In lakes and reservoirs of Southern Europe, techniques have been developed for prebaiting that were unimaginable to the pioneers on small English fishing waters. A boat is used to row out both the prebait and the bait. The fishing can be done at distances of over 400 m (1300 ft). To find the way back to the prebaiting spot, a marker is set out, such as an empty bottle.

Marker advantages

Markers are beneficial in all waters. They show exactly how the prebaits are distributed. You then know, instead of only guessing, when the bait lies just right. In waters with much vegetation, there may be areas of half a square meter that are free and perfect for the hook bait.

By using floats with a light stave, a marker works just as well at night, when it would otherwise be impossible to cast out quite correctly.

Surface fishing

Bottom angling is the predominant method of carp fishing (see tackle and principles in the chapter on bottom angling). But under special conditions, when the fish swim high in the water, opportunities for surface fishing arise. If the fish go really near land, one can fish with only a hook on the end of the line.

'Controller'

Usually a special float called a 'controller' is needed. It is weighted so as to protrude only about a centimeter above the

Below: A broad-gap, rather thin hook, such as the Drennan Wide Gape Specialist, is a perfect bread hook.

Carp fishing offers fine close battles like bullfighting.

surface, where the line glides through its top. The controller provides both casting weight and a way of keeping the line properly stretched. The leader length depends on how shy the fish are. A good starting length is 1.5 m (5 ft)

Baits: bread

Bread is among the simplest and best surface baits. If carp stand still, or slowly cruise under the surface, it is suitable to throw out some pieces of bread. Few things can make one as nervous as when the pouting mouth of a 10 kg (20 lb) smacking carp sucks in the bread and comes ever closer to the piece with the hook. If the fish takes the bait, one must keep a cool head. The commonest cause of a missed catch, when surface fishing, is that you strike back too soon. This is almost a spinal reflex when the bait is sucked in, but you have to wait. And when you feel ready to hook, wait a little longer. Even though I know this, on several occasions I have pulled the bait out of the mouth of a big carp that took me hours to lure in for taking it.

Baits: cat and dog food

Other surface-fishing baits are floating cat and dog food. Since the pieces are small, a similar effect is achieved with them as when fishing with particle baits. The fish eat many of them and become less suspicious. With smooth, patient work it is possible to get a whole group of carp to eat them, which amplifies the effect. The more are eating, the more they compete, and the easier they are to fool. When five or six carp suck in bait after bait, cruising like mini-submarines in the surface layer, the time is right to lay out the hook bait carefully. With polarized glasses and a sharp eye, you will also have seen which fish is biggest and can focus on catching it.

Fishing in the margins

From surface fishing, there is only a short step to sneak-fishing, just below the rod tip, and out to a few rod lengths away. Here is a recollection from carp fishing somewhere. It has begun to grow light when I arrive.

I let down the gear ten metres from the shore, put together the ready-tackled rod and start to sneak forward. On my knees I approach the edge of reeds. With a metre to the water, I settle myself and lob out the tackle. The float lands with a little splash. Cautiously I lay down the rod so that it rests in the reeds and sticks out a metre. Around the float I throw a couple of handfuls of corn.

Bubbles and spatter

Suddenly some bubbles rise near the float, and my pulse goes up. What was that? A slight shake of the float top. The float shakes again and is pulled under at an angle. I hook when it disappears. Two metres out, the water explodes. I stand up and get splashed, then hold on with all my might. At first I think I have stopped the fish, but it makes only a pause under the rod tip before taking off. The reel screams as the fish madly tears out line. Only when it has taken twenty metres do I put a stop to the beast, despite holding on so hard that the rod creaks. It goes up with a powerful whirl in the midst of a thick pondweed belt. There I had lost two fish the previous morning.

I am fishing alone, and the bottom has a metre-thick layer of sediment, so I do not dare to wade after the fish. If one's feet get stuck there, one stays put. Instead I try to bring the fish in. With the rod pointing straight toward it, I back up very slowly. It follows for five metres, like a nice big dog on a leash, before it has had enough. There is a huge splash and it frees itself from the hook. After winding in the tackle, I still have water dripping from my glasses and the pondweed is swaying in the swell.

Magical shores

The fishing that season was to demonstrate what I already knew – how good the area along the shore is. In five attempts, of some hours each, I got around twenty bites, and landed seven. Despite an effort to hold the fish hard after each bite, to prevent them from rushing into the vegetation, I failed. Of the first six bites, I lost five before learning from my mistakes. None of the fish took the bait farther from land than five metres – most took it only a rod length out, and a couple less than a metre out.

The fishing took place in a lake that covered three hectares, but the magic of the shore is equally strong in larger lakes. In a lake that measures 350 hectares, all of my carp have come up less than four metres from land, even though I was fishing at the same time with at least one tackle as far out as fifty metres. Here, precision fishing at overhanging branches or along the shore's sloping rocky edges has been very effective.

The lake's larder

It is not surprising that shore fishing should be so good. Where land meets water, there is a constant inflow of fish food to the lake. Rain washes down insects and worms; bugs are continually falling into the water from branches and other plants. The shore is simply the best-filled larder in most lakes. From a fisherman's viewpoint, it cannot be better. Placing a bait perfectly under the rod tip is also easier than laying it on a shallow plateau or a deep cliff thirty metres out – whose exact position you first have to find.

Matched tackle

Adeptness with such large fish, in waters murky with vegetation, calls for equipment with the right combination of strength and softness. If the fish gains speed, it usually gets away, so the tactic is to hook and hold on for dear life. Then the line cannot be too weak – 0.30 mm (0.01 in) is a minimum – or the rod too inflexible. Otherwise there is a risk of the line snapping or the hook being torn out. A rod of 12–13 feet with full action is ideal. It works softly and has reserve strength even when bent down to the handle.

With a small bag for snacks, bait, slingshot, carp bag, and tackle items over your back, a net in one hand and the rod in the other, you are ready to sneak along the shore. Far from traditional carp fishing with a rod bag, carp bed, sleeping bag and alarm, this is fishing for close encounters and battles with creatures of 10–15 kilo (22-30 lbs), the bullfights of the carp arena.

Tench

Tench are among our most handsome and exciting candidates for angling. They vary from shimmering olive-green to flaming orange, with watchful ruby-red eyes. Strongly reminiscent of carp, they have a similar body form and another mysterious reputation.

Tench fishing extends over the whole spectrum of angling methods, but has increasingly shifted towards a scaled-down carp technique with boilies. In some waters, this has given the fishing a renaissance – when boilies are introduced, it often becomes ever better.

The minimal carp method

Small soft boilies

Carp techniques for tench are like those for their namesake, but there are crucial differences. In particular, the boilies that are used should be 10–14 mm (0.4-0.5 in) wide, instead of the carp's standard 16–22 mm (0.6-0.8 in). And a key factor is the consistency. Carp boilies can be as hard as pebbles and still catch fish. Tench boilies must be softer. If fish such as chub and roach did not also like small, soft, tasty balls, the ideal would be boilies so soft that they nearly mash when picked up.

It is troublesome to roll mini-boilies, but as long as the bait industry does not supply consumers with soft boilies, there is no option. Roll up your sleeves, bring out bowls and pots, flour blends and flasks of scent and start rolling.

Tackle

The tackle is the same as for carp. I have had most success with firm bolt rigs of the 'straight' type – with the sinker locked on the line and the leader in front. The leader must be shorter than for carp, about 15 cm (0.5 ft), and its material the softest, most flexible available.

For carp, short hair is needed to attach the boilie at the hook. For tench, I use even shorter hair. It is hard to knot hair rigs of 14–15 mm (0.5 in), but it pays off. A bolt rig with a short leader, very short hair, and mini-boilies is superb. The bites literally explode.

Float angling

The lift method. A traditional approach to tench is angling with an antenna float and the lift method (see the section on

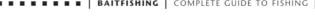

Top: Tench vary from deep olive-green to flaming orange, with a ruby-red eye like the dot over the 'i'.

Bottom: *Dawn is the primary time for tench.*

float angling). The float is fished over-deep, with a sinker on the bottom so that the bites – when the fish takes up the bait and sinker – will make the float rise. The distance between the shot and the hook is varied until you find one where the bites are clear and the strike yields a hooked fish. Begin with 10 cm (4 in).

Over vegetation

In the water above vegetation, it is necessary to fish differently. The float is adjusted so that the bait hangs just over the plants, easy for fish to see and with no risk of hooking rubbish.

Traditional bottom angling

Bottom angling with paternoster tackle and swimfeeder is also effective for tench. The leader is kept quite short to get the hook bait just at the edge of the feeder's chum pile. A variant is to combine a maggot with a maggot-filled feeder closed at both ends, instead of an open one with maggots and bread chum.

With this technique, fishermen often use two hook leaders so as to fish with different baits. In my opinion, such a procedure is not beneficial. Tench fishing commonly occurs near vegetation and the risk is that a second leader will snag after a bite, resulting in a lost fish.

Choice of place and prebaiting

The place. Where to fish for tench is determined by the same factors as in carp fishing. Here too, it is a matter of finding the hot bottom structures. The difference is that tench are more partial to vegetation.

The prebait. Prebaiting with boilies is done as with carp. It can be advantageous to begin by also using breadcrumbs, which attract the fish rapidly. You may, of course, design prebaiting campaigns for traditional baits too, but these attract other fish as well. Thus, the choice is often to prebait during the fishing itself – with bread crumbs if the fishing is done far from land, or by loosefeeding if you fish near land or from a boat.

Particle boilies

A special variant is fishing with boilies and particle baits made of boilie paste. Then you use a spod (see the section on pre-

baiting) to create a sparse carpet of small baits around the hook bait, or a plastic bag filled with small baits and tied to the tackle.

Traditional baits

Worms, maggots and bread are among the best baits for tench, my favorites being earthworms. Many a tench is also taken on corn – but just like carp, tench learn rapidly from their mistakes.

The English tench guru Len Head writes, in his book Tench, that corn often works well at first, but that the fish soon become suspicious. He describes the result: "Lightning-quick bites on the float tackle, hardly leaving time to hook the fish.

Opposite:
Top: Fishing with small boilies and scaled-down carp technique is hard to beat for catching tench.
Bottom: Just like carp fishermen, the tench fisherman carefully returns the fish to the water.

Below: Boilies for tench should be small and soft, and the leader material flexible.

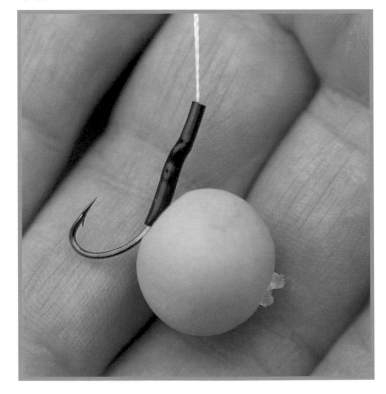

When the tench swim over dense vegetation, the solution may be float angling with the bait set to fish over the plants.

And the fisherman's experience the following morning, when he discovers that tench under cover of darkness have cleaned out the chubbing spot of every corn but one, the one with the hook in it."

Flavoring

A way to lengthen the life of corn bait is to color and flavor it. The fish will then regard it as new bait, and can temporarily be as 'easy to catch' as when the corn was fresh in the water. A fisherman can also improve his chances relative to others by adding a taste of his own. The same is true when fishing with boilies. Examples of good tastes are almond, kiwi and banana.

Equipment

Boilie fishing

Ideal tench rods for boilie fishing are of the carp model, 11 feet (3.3 m) long and half-action. On such gear, hooked tench give real fights that are pure enjoyment. Most of them take off on a first sizzling rush then change between fast sidewise attacks and bullish dives toward the bottom. The reels are the same as for carp fishing.

Float and bottom angling

For traditional bottom angling, the usual equipment of 11–12 feet (3.5 m) is used. I prefer a swingtip rod, since the bites often need to be waited out. For float angling, thicker match rods of 13–14 feet (4 m) are perfect. The line must be 0.22 - 0.25 mm (0.08-0.01 in) thick, as the fishing often takes place in vegetation.

Tips on drilling

Frequently a tench rushes away, just after biting, straight into the nearest pondweed belt or reed bed. If so, you should let enough line out to hang in an arc from the rod. Give the fish time – several minutes may pass, but it usually emerges again. When the line begins to move, you need only resume the pressure. In this way, nine out of ten hooked tench can be dealt with.

Bream

Tips on prebaiting

Prebaiting is essential for maintenance of bream fishing, and its principles are simple. Moisten some bread chum and mix it with well-known bream magnets such as maggots, corn and worms. The mixture is formed into tangerine-sized balls that are delivered with a slingshot to the fishing spot. In summer, ten to fifteen balls are a good start.

Bream love sweets. Vanilla sugar is a fine, cheap additive. Super-sweet ones in powder form are nice but costlier. Effective flavors are vanilla, cola, cream-like tastes, and the strong sweet one of molasses. Concentrated flavorings or sweeteners in liquid form can be added to the water that the bread crumb is moistened with.

Technique

The standard method for bream is bottom angling with a paternoster tackle. The hook leader should be about a meter long, and the sinker leader 40 cm (1,3ft). Instead of a sinker, a swimfeeder can be used, but this is desirable mainly when the water is relatively cold, as the fish then need much less food.

Equipment

Quivertip

A quivertip or swingtip rod of 11 feet (3.35 m) is ideal. With the quivertip a bite tends to begin with some brief tugs, then the tip is bent softly and stubbornly. Only at that point should you hook the fish strongly.

Swingtip

Unless the current or distance is against it, I use a swingtip. After casting and tensing up the line, the rod hangs obliquely downward instead of tensely. A bite is shown by a rise or fall of the tip. The resistance does not increase when the line is stretched, and there can be a longer wait before the fish feels any resistance. This last advantage can make the difference between good fishing and frustrating attempts to hook fish.

Reel, line and hook

A spinning reel with line of 0.18–0.20 mm (0.007 in) suits the rods and the fishing. Nylon line is best, since bream swim

Above: *Bottom angling with a swingtip for bream is a great summer pleasure.*

Top right: *A large bream arches to the surface.*

Bottom right: *Finding a bream school and prebaiting correctly can yield true action.*

in schools and a flat line produces many more false signals from fish running into it. Sinkers that weigh 15–25 g (0.7 oz) cover most situations. The hook is selected according to the bait's size, 10–12 being good for several corn grains, a bunch of maggots or a big caterpillar. Hook sizes of 12–14 are appropriate for smaller bait: a couple of maggots, one or two corn grains or a small caterpillar. Combine the baits and test them until the bites come fast.

Right: A big bream on its way into the net.

Opposite:
Top: Worms, corn, maggots and casters – these are candy for bream.
Bottom: Hold the fish by its tail spool and lay it in the water.

Choosing the place

It is important to choose the right place, even though fish must be attracted there by prebaiting. To prebait where no fish pass by is as silly as fishing on dry land. Often the best approach is to fish in the wind.

In most lakes the bream follow definite routes when seeking food. These are often connected with deep cliffs at the transition to flatter bottoms. Here, bottom material accumulates and creates good conditions for the favorite food of bream: water-dwelling worms (the freshwater cousins of earthworms) and fly larvae. Such cliffs are found by sounding. At or just outside the edge is where you should cast out the prebait and fish. In flowing waters, schools of bream patrol the calm sections.

Tactics

Cast out to the far side of the prebaited area. Let the bait lie for some minutes, pull it in half a meter, tighten up and wait a few more minutes, before retrieving the tackle. Often the bite comes after an inward pull. Wait till the swingtip is lifted, or the quivertip is bent considerably. Hook the fish and feel the thrill of the first solid resistance. I wonder how many times a fish weighing a kilogram has convinced me that something much bigger has taken the bait.

As long as the bites keep coming within a few minutes of the cast, it is best not to prebait any more – this frequently frightens the fish rather than attracting them. The best time to do so is when the bites have almost ceased. Then the fish are departing, or else the school has mostly been fished up, and further food will revive their interest or prepare for the next school.

If no bites come immediately, and they seldom do, it is advisable to cast out a little ball of chum every quarter or half hour, to keep a scent of food in the water above and around the chumming spot, so that fish are drawn there faster.

Chub

Surface fishing

The summer technique of floating-bread fishing is difficult to beat. With a soft rod, preferably of the match type at 12–13 feet (3.5–4 m), and a single hook on a 0.16 mm (0.006 in) line, you are ready. Somewhat longer casts are obtained by dipping the bread piece for an instant in the water. To fish at greater distances, towards the other side of a small stream, for instance, a controller is tied on (see the section about carp). The most important tip is to delay the strike until the line is stretched.

Bottom angling

For chub, the most common method is bottom angling with a quiver rod of 11–12 feet (3.5 m) and paternoster tackle. The sinker is determined by the current conditions (see the previous section on bottom angling). A swimfeeder loaded with bread chum and small bread flakes can be worth trying, if you sit a little longer at a particularly profitable holding place. Once cast out, the swimfeeder contents more or less explode, and fluffy bread bits whirl with the current, attracting fish that stand downstream to bite eagerly.

Baits

White bread is one of the best baits. It smells good and, in bottom angling, it floats a little upward to move attractively in the current. Cheese, both in pure form and as paste, is another classic. Corn has yielded many chub, as have chickpeas and other particle baits. Pieces of sausage, luncheon meat, shrimp and snails – the chub benefits from anything edible. It pays to vary the baits, since they are usually most effective at the start.

The best hook for large baits such as bread, cheese and shrimp is a broad-gapped, thin, chemically polished model of size 2–4.

Holding places

Chub are a species for flowing waters. During summer, they are found in the fastest parts of the current – behind or beneath fallen branches, under overhanging trees, and within the bottom current's channels between waving wreaths of vegetation. They are often in surprisingly shallow water, which gives them an excellent position for taking food that comes swirling along. Then they rise, suck it in, and return to shelter.

Their winter holding places are often deeper, in more calmly flowing water. They hold still behind or below branches, trees

Above: In the summer, chub keep to the strong currents and linger under branches, in channels among vegetation, and at other sheltered spots.
Top centre: Cheese can be fished in either piece or paste form.
Top right: During the winter, calm backwaters are preferred by chub.
Bottom right: A large mouth and black-edged scales are hallmarks of chub.

and the like. While they now seldom hold in the fastest current, it is usually not far away.

Mobility is superiority

A key to success is to vary your location. Walk along a fair stretch and fish for ten to thirty minutes, then move to the next possible holding place. Any bites will be hard and hungry, almost heart-stopping. The rod may be nearly ripped away, though generally after a few short shocks of warning. In the winter, it can be rewarding to try a little longer at a good place, since the fish there may need more time.

Night fishing

The best time for big fish is during the first hours after nightfall, regardless of whether in summer or winter. But especially during the summer, fishing all night is a smart investment.

Roach

Roach is a classic species for the angler. Most of us come into contact with it through our first attempts to fish during childhood, and it often yields the bulk of the fish in angling competitions. Before the carp boom a big roach was one of the specimen fisherman's most desirable trophies. While a roach of only 900 g (1.8 lb) is considered large, this fish is a worthy opponent. Pugnacious and tricky, it can be caught all year round, with all methods of angling.

Method

Float angling. Trotting with a stick float, combined with loosefeeding, was developed largely for catching roach. The tackle is as light a stick float as possible, with the shot spread out on the line so that bites are seen clearly 'on the drop', as the fish may be holding anywhere between the bottom and the surface.

Loosefeeding

The fisherman shoots or throws out some maggots, casters or hemp corn, and lets the tackle wander with them downstream. Now and then the tackle is held back carefully so that the bait rises. If no bites come, the tackle is adjusted so that the bait fishes closer to the bottom or surface. This is done by moving the sinker downward or upward, combined with setting the float deeper or more shallowly. Often the fish rise ever higher in the water and the float has to be fished more shallowly.

The top knot

For the top knot, the tackle builds on the same principle, with the sinker weight evenly spread from the depth where the fish are expected to be, down to the signal shot nearest the hook. With the top knot, the fisherman can follow the tackle exactly and, since it is more sensitive than reel-rod tackle, it works better on cautious fish.

Bottom angling

Closed swimfeeder. In still waters, bottom angling with a swimfeeder on a paternoster tackle is excellent for large roach. During the day, the fish often swim into deeper water, which calls for longer casts. With a swimfeeder, the prebaiting is always perfect. Frequently it is best to avoid bread chum and load only with hook baits, because bread does not attract small roach. The fishing is then done with a closed swimfeeder, which

Float angling and loosefeeding with maggots or corn is a classic method for roach.

has no openings in the ends. It is loaded with maggots and closed by a lid. The baits crawl out through small holes.

Open swimfeeder

The alternative is a little bread chum, as plugs in an open feeder. You can then use other baits than those that crawl out by themselves. Examples are corn and casters – maggot larvae. The latter are known for attracting big roaches and can float. A couple of casters on a thin hook of size 14, with a leader of thin line, lifts a little from the bottom and is seen better by the fish. Another classic big-roach bait consists of some white bread crumb squeezed around the hook. A hook size of 6–10 is then adequate.

Fishing by dark

Bottom angling with a paternoster is also best for nocturnal fishing in flowing waters. A leader length of around one meter to the hook, and 20–30 cm (0.6-0.9 ft)) to the sinker, is a good starting-point. If the fish are hard to hook, there are two solutions. Lengthen the leader until the bites are reached, or use a really short leader of 20–30 cm (0.6-0.9 ft) so that the fish hooks itself against the sinker. The latter is usually most effective in the dark.

Roach often provide the bulk of the weight in angling contests.

Equipment

A light match rod about 13 feet (4 m) long is ideal. For bottom angling, an 11-foot (3.3 m) quiver rod with a soft top is used. The line should be thin, 0.12–0.15 mm (0.005 in). Thicker line is used in water where the risk is great that the fish will get stuck, or when fishing at a long distance.

Prebaiting

If you fish with bait, it is good to mix small pieces in the prebait. Hemp, both mashed and whole, is another magnet for roach. If bread chum is used, one does well to fish with a 'lift bait' – casters or bread – over a sparse carpet of chum.

Where to fish

Flowing waters. In flowing waters roach are found at the edges between stronger and weaker currents. The stronger the current, or the colder the water, the more the fish move into calm backwaters. Also rewarding are the insides of curves, from a third of the stream's width out to the middle. In summertime, the fish may linger in strong currents of shallow water, preferably among stretches of swaying vegetation.

Still waters. Roach swim along both the upper and lower parts of submerged cliffs, and especially on the shelves if any exist. They also stand along reeds and other vegetation edges, as well as near the inlets and outlets of streams. In both still and flowing waters, the fishing is often good next to, or above, gravelly sections. Places with an onshore wind are best unless it is really cold.

When to fish

In wintertime the fishing is normally best during the lighter hours of the day. But the rest of the fishing season is different. For large roach, night fishing is preferable, notably during the first hours after dark falls and the last hours before dawn. In lakes, the fish then approach shore to eat, which makes them easier both to reach and to trick. Yet in flowing waters, too, the chances are greatest of catching big fish when it is dark.

Rudd

Bottom angling. With its underbite and close-set eyes high on the head, a rudd looks like a fish that takes food from below. In spite of this, many large rudd are caught by bottom angling. Why? One of the most effective techniques is fishing with big pieces of bread that float upward in the water. The leader length is chosen so that the bait stays near the surface, even though the sinker remains on the bottom. At a depth of just over a meter, a leader of 1.5 m (5 ft) is enough in flowing waters – for deeper water, the leader is longer. The tackle is an ordinary paternoster.

Float angling
In flowing waters

Diverse forms of float angling are also effective, such as classic Avon or stick-float fishing with loosefeeding of corn or maggots. In this case, you should fish with the float adjusted so that the bait rises a little in the water. Restrain and release the line so that the bait lifts and falls, a movement that attracts the fish in free water.

A variant is an Avon float that carries plenty of weight, combined with large bread baits. The weight is then set two-thirds of the way down on the tackle, and must be great enough to sink the bread. Fished a little down in the water, the bait covers considerably wider areas than if it were bottom-angled.

In still waters

A technique appropriate to still waters is a light stick float tackled 'top-bottom', with the sinkers collected directly under the float to provide casting weight. With baits that float or fall very slowly, this tackle suits fish that want their bait high in the water. At longer distances, a light controller and long leader are used.

Tackle

Rudd are fighters and make determined rushes, but are not giants. Quivertip rods of 11 feet (3.3 m), for casting weights around 20 g (0.7 oz) and a line of 0.15–0.16 mm (0.005 in), or lighter match rods with line of 0.14–0.16 mm (0.005 in), are perfect.

Prebaiting

Besides loosefeeding in float angling, a swimfeeder is an established aid to catching rudd. When bread is the bait, the feeder is fished in the same way as for chub. It is loaded with bread chum and small bread bits that drift with the current.

Baits
Bread

The rudd's miniature mouth makes it easy to underestimate the size of the bait, but rudd that weigh over a kilogram take bigger bait – up to half the size of a matchbox. This may be because they use their sight to find food, and a larger bait is easier to see. For such big bait, you need hooks of sizes 4–6 with a wide gap and thin metal, sharp as a needle. Desirable, too, is a little barb to penetrate better, as on Drennan's 'Wide Gape Specialist', my favorite for bread baits.

Floating alternatives

It can pay off to try other floating baits, obeying the same principles as for bread. Small floating boilies on a hair rig, or pieces that keep a couple of corn grains floating, are examples. Their aroma is also attractive, and can be varied if the fish lose interest. One variant is to lay maggots in the water. These begin to float after a while, and a bunch on a thin-shafted hook will stand up in the water like a piece of bread.

Bottom baits

Despite their appearance, rudd are caught on the bottom as well. Other good baits are worms, corn and maggots when fished traditionally.

Place

Rudd are found in the richly vegetated coves of lakes, and in calmly flowing backwaters of streams. They prefer to linger alongside or inside the plant stands. In the evening, they enter very shallow water.

Time

It is possible to catch rudd at all times of year when the water is open, but the biggest ones are usually caught early in springtime. Night fishing is extremely productive, and my comrades and I have frequently fished along stretches that seemed totally lifeless until the arrival of dark set the bites going.

Opposite. Top left: With float angling and baits such as bread, maggot and corn, the quieter parts of streams can be effectively fished out.
Top right: Blood-red fins are characteristic of rudd.
Bottom: The goldfish of the lake, caught on bottom-angled bread.

Pike angling
Ordinary float angling

Modern angling is not just a hunt for big carpfish – it is also one of the very best weapons for coming into contact with predatory fish such as pike, pikeperch, perch and sheatfish. Among these, the pike is the most popular species, and many of the techniques have been developed for this type of fishing in particular.

Tackle

A carp rod of 11–12 feet (3.5 m) is ideal for pike angling. It facilitates casting out the small, clumsy tackles, keeping good line control, and taking up slack line before hooking. And the rod has the power that is needed to drive the hook into a pike's bony jaw and to steer the fish while playing it.

Leader

The leader should not be of nylon. This material suits small pike but the leader can break when a dream fish shows up.
A leader at least 40 cm (1 ft) long is needed. Best make your own, which is simpler than it sounds. There are several good wire materials on sale, such as Drennan's Sevenstrand or Pikewire. The instructions are on the package.

Up-trace

Preferably one should have an 'up-trace', which is an extra leader above the hook leader. This prevents the pike from reaching and cutting the line over the leader. An example is when the tackle is fished a little above the bottom, as in angling for pelagic pike. Then the bite often comes from below, and the pike can easily catch the line in its jaw during the attack. When fishing in flowing waters, the sinker is frequently set only a few centimeters over the bottom, and baitfish swim at that level or higher up in the water. The risk of the line coming into contact with pike teeth is thus great. The same is true if baitfish have wound the leader around the main line.

With a length of about a meter on the up-trace, there is almost no danger of having the main line cut. Since the sinkers should sit just over the hook leader, you can make several up-traces with different weights, adapted to floats with different bearing weights – or use sinkers of 'Catherine' type, which can be attached according to the weight required.

Left: All that is needed to rig for pike angling. Wire, sleeve, hook and pliers for leaders, floats, sinkers, and plastic beads to mount between sinker and leader, as well as between stop-knot and float.

Right: Ready for pike angling. An adaptable float, leader, and plastic bead between stop-knot and float, so that the knot does not slip through the float – and one beyond the sinker, tied to the swivel that holds the leader, so that the knot is protected. The roach is rigged with one hook in its back before the dorsal fin, and one at the breast fin.

Hook

I prefer a pair of treble hooks. The strike can then be applied immediately, minimizing the risk of hooking a pike in the throat. Forget ideas such as delaying the strike for ten minutes – or as I read somewhere in my youth: lighting a cigarette, smoking it up, and finally hooking – to make sure that the pike has the hooks in its mouth. This is absurd. It makes smoking harmful not only to the fisherman, but also to the fish.

Size 6 is adequate for the biggest pike. Models with small barbs, or with barbs squeezed in towards the shaft with pliers, are easy to loosen.

Tackling on

The baitfish's size determines the distance between the treble hooks on a leader; it should be between 10 and 15 cm (4.5 in). The baitfish is tackled differently depending on whether the fishing is done in lakes or flowing waters. In lake fishing – where the baitfish should swim around the boat, or the place on land where you stand – the upper hook is fastened at the fish's dorsal fin, and the lower hook in its mouth or at a breast fin.

In flowing waters, the upper hook should sit in the mouth, and the lower hook either at the dorsal fin or between the breast fin and anal fin. The fish then adopts a natural movement in the water, and is not dragged crosswise through the water when it is reeled in.

Floats

A sliding float that is stopped with a stop-knot on the line makes depth adjustments simple. A plastic bead between the knot and float decreases the danger of the knot getting stuck in the float or sliding through. I use as light a float as possible, so as to hold up the tackle and baitfish. Use a cigar-shaped float of around 20 g (0.7oz), made of lead, so that it sticks up one or two centimeters.

Top left: With a small aquarium net, baitfish are easy to lift from a bucket.
Bottom left: A quick strike usually puts the hooks in the corner of the fish's mouth – where they sit securely and are easy to loosen.

Line control

Line control is the A and Z. When a pike bites, the line should not be slack. Otherwise the fish may spit out the bait before you are ready to hook, or may have time to swallow the hooks deeply while you reel in. With a fairly taut line, the strike is simple. Point the rod tip toward the fish, reel until you feel resistance, and then strike hard. With a braided line on the reel, the hook will sit tight.

Play it calmly

Take it easy with a hooked fish, if you are not in a spot where it can get stuck. With moderate pressure, you have all the cards in your hand. Preferably, a pike should not be taken so hard that it flies up and shakes its head. This stresses the hooking and tackle so much that it may shake itself loose. A net is an obvious necessity, and ought to be a large one. During pike fishing, a dream fish can take the bait at any time. Keep cool when the fish is ready for the net. Hold the net in the water with its front edge under the surface, lead the fish over it, and lift.

Place

Places for pike angling in flowing waters have been mentioned. In lakes and along coasts, the pike may hold at edges of vegetation, at submerged cliffs – to be fished from the upper to the lower edge – and at reefs or outlets. An echo sounder makes it easy to find bottom structures and schools of baitfish. Where they are, the pike are. Bait just over the bottom is a good beginning, but fishing in free water can be needed to attract pelagic fish such as herring, vendace or smelt.

When the baitfish are hard to locate, or are spread out so that it is difficult to prefer any special place, an advantage lies in turning to mobile pike angling – float trolling.

Float trolling

Rowing with one or two baitfish after the boat – float trolling – is not only as good as the more traditional stationary pike angling, but often far more effective. Basically it is a simple method that has been developed into a fine weapon for hunting large pike.

One of my fishing companions, who has caught (and returned) thousands of angled pike, summed up float trolling like this: "Go with a braided line, fish at depths between two and six meters, and keep the bait at the bottom – you'll catch fish." A good description of the method, but there is certainly more to its effectiveness.

Echo sounder

Bait at the bottom is a fundamental rule with no exceptions. In waters where the pike hunt pelagically, or during the autumn when the baitfish may be holding anywhere in the water volume after autumn mixes it, the quarry may need to be fished at other depths. An echo sounder is thus almost indispensable for successful float trolling. It keeps track of the water depth, cliff edges, shallows and so forth, as well as finding baitfish. Finding schools of baitfish with the help of an echo sounder is often more profitable than aimlessly fishing across a lake in the hope of eventually hitting the target.

Tackle

Rod, reel, line

You can use an ordinary spinning or baitcasting rod, but a carp rod of 11–12 feet (3.5 m) is also preferable for float trolling. Besides having enough spine to drive in the hook, it has a length that enables the tackle to be guided far to the sides for broad fishing. With a baitrunner function on the reel, the risk is avoided of losing your whole bait set-up to a fast bite. As in ordinary pike angling, an inflexible braided line is superior.

Choose an ample net.

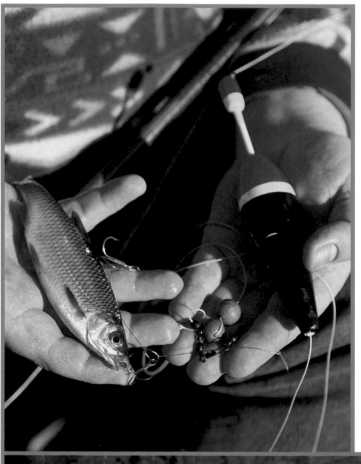

Floats

There are special floats for float trolling, but they are not really needed. An ordinary gliding pike float threaded on the line works perfectly. The special floats are designed not to slide down on the line with the boat's motion, but normally one does not row so fast that this happens with an ordinary float. If it should turn out that the fish on a given day want a faster bait, or if you fish while rowing against the current in flowing waters, the float can be secured with a loosely tied stop-knot below it. This should sit so loosely that the float can easily be pressed down along the line, in cases where you fish deeper than three-fourths of a rod length, since it may then be necessary to reel in more line when a fish is to be netted.

Slow pace

Often the key to success is slow motion. If the float slides down the line, it usually means you are moving too fast. Take a pull on the oars, rest till the boat almost stops, take another and let the boat stop completely, and so on. The reason

Top left: In float trolling, as when angling in flowing waters, the roach should be tackled with the upper hook in its mouth and the rear hook at a breast fin.

Below: Float trolling comes into its own during the colder seasons.

Smaller pike can be held by gripping the upper neck when the hook is removed.

why slow rowing seems to be the winning tune is presumably that float trolling is practiced mainly during the period from autumn until spring. But obviously your speed may need to be varied, and on certain days a much quicker pace may be required to attract bites. The rowing itself gives a varied speed that makes baitfish rise and fall in the water with the strokes. This is one explanation for the fact that float trolling is some-times much more effective than plain stationary angling.

Leader and 'up-trace'

The same leaders are used as in ordinary pike angling – and especially when going after pelagic fish, an up-trace is essential.

Rigging

The lowermost hook is fastened either in the baitfish's back at the dorsal fin, or at one lateral fin, and the other hook in the mouth. Then the baitfish swims, or is pulled, through the water headfirst. A hook at the breast fin also works as a kind of keep and holds the baitfish upright in the water.

Tactics

The success of float trolling is largely a result of the fisher-man's effective coverage of much greater areas than in ordi-nary pike angling. With an echo sounder, submerged cliffs are found that can be followed with a tackle fished in the upper

In late autumn, winter and early spring, most fish are caught by slow back trolling with pike-angling tackle.

edge and another, deeper tackle farther out. The next rowing tour can be done farther out on the cliff side, or closer to land or the shallows. When seeking pelagic fish, the baits are set at different depths in relation to how the schools of baitfish show up on the sounder.

Unless a pattern emerges after a few bites and the tackles can be fished more similarly, different variants must be tested until the fish loosen up.

A trump in the hand of a float-trolling ace is to row over a hot spot not just once, but also backward to get the bait to a pike's assumed holding place, two or three times. In this way the technique becomes a real skill, where the distinction between untouched bait and a diving float may be only meters.

Place

As in ordinary pike angling, the aim is to fish in the areas where fish are holding, and the places are the same as when fishing from an anchored boat or from land. Float trolling, however, is mainly a technique for still waters. Boat fishing in a stream or river works better in a reverse variant – back trolling.

Back trolling
The art form of pike angling

This special form of pike angling, or float trolling, can be called back trolling since the name rather well describes what it is about. In flowing water, the fisherman slowly releases the boat downstream with one or two pike tackles drifting before it. The technique is ideally suited for long areas with reed-edged stream or river stretches, or along cliffs toward the deep furrow.

When done by an old hand, it looks simple, but it takes time to learn. There is nothing easy about holding a boat against the current so that the tackle works downstream with the right speed and depth.

Depth adjustment

Since the fisherman is holding the boat back, the current presses on the line, and this must be kept in mind when the depth is set. Some over-depth, or extra distance between the float and sinker than the water depth, is needed so that the

How smart is it to fish with anything but a steel leader for these pike?

tackle with baitfish will not rise too high in the water when the boat is kept still or is slowly braked downstream.

'Overleading'

In truly strong current, the sinker weight may have to exceed what the float would tolerate if fishing in still waters. As the fisherman holds back, the current lifts the tackle and the float climbs a bit, so that it stands at a moderate depth without being pulled under.

Extra stop-knot

Tying an extra stop-knot below the float may be necessary, to prevent the current from pressing it down on the line. The knot should be fairly loose, so that the float can be forced down on the line when the playing is finished with the netting.

Equipment
Rod

The rods are the same as in ordinary pike angling: carp rods 11–12 feet long (3.5 m). Some float trollers manage to fish with two rods, but others prefer a single one. The reason is that, as already noted, it is hard to handle the boat with the current at the right speed, so that the tackle drifts properly in relation to the water depth.

Reel

So as not to risk losing the rod at the bite, or in case the boat rushes away downstream when the fisherman is busy with one or two rods, it is best to fish with a spinning reel that has a baitrunner function.

Tackle and rigging

The leader and up-trace are the same as float trolling and ordinary pike angling. The baitfish is rigged just as when angling in flowing waters. The leader's lower treble hook is placed at the fish's dorsal fin or one abdominal fin, and the other hook in its mouth. Then the fish will always be oriented against the current, as if it were swimming freely.

The bite

A bite is felt when the float is clearly drawn under the surface, tips to the side, or slowly sinks as if the tackle has snagged on the bottom. Then you should strike, preferably without the boat drifting away downstream.

Ice along the river edges did not stop this huge pike from plucking up the tackled smelt.

Reed stop or emergency anchoring

A means of preventing the boat from drifting away is to open your bail when the fish bites, so that line can be pulled easily off the reel. Next, row a few strokes toward land, if possible into reeds if they grow along the edge, where the boat will lie more still. Then reel in line until you feel resistance, and make your strike. With the boat in the reeds, you have a good position to play and net the fish without problems. The alternative is to keep the anchor in the prow, tied to the boat with adequate line length for the fishing depth, and ready to be thrown in at a second's notice.

Bottom Angling
Free line and sliding tackle

Particularly in England, it is also common to bottom-angle for pike, sometimes while prebaiting with pieces of fish. The simplest technique is with a free line or an ordinary sliding bottom tackle. By threading a swivel with a snap onto the line, the sinker weight can be changed quickly for adaptation to the casting length or the current.

Bait

The most usual bait is a piece of, or even an entire, dead baitfish. It may be either a species natural to the water – roach, rudd, smelt, eel or the like – or a bit of some other fish: mackerel, herring or sardine. Fatty fish, such as the last five mentioned, are notably attractive when their scent spreads in the water.

Leader and rigging

The leader is determined by the baitfish's size, but normally a leader with two treble hooks is used. Given a whole baitfish, the lower hook is set above its breast fins, and the other hook farther up toward the tail. Then the tackle casts best. Half a fish is attached with the broader end at the lower hook, and the other a little way up. To prevent them from flying off in the cast, large baits are secured with a piece of PVA tied round the bait and the leader slightly up from the hooks, or with a rubber band in the same position.

Floating paternoster

One can use live baitfish on a sliding tackle, but there are better solutions. Most common is a variant of the paternoster tackle, where a float is somewhat up the line and lifts the bait-fish in the water. The leader sits in a three-way swivel 1–1.5 meters (5 ft) up from the sinker. Between the leader and main line is an up-trace, as described above.

Depth adjustment

The float is placed so that the distance between it and the sinker exceeds the water depth. Then the tackle can be 'tightened up' against the sinker for rapid registering of bites.

Rod holder

Usually one fishes with several rods in holders including bite indicators.

Place

Since bottom angling is a stationary technique, it becomes most effective during the cold months of the year. Good places in rivers and streams are the backwaters and current edges – or in lakes, the level bottom below cliffs, the vicinity of vegetation belts, at inlets and outlets.

With equipment on a sledge, and an ice-pick in hand to test where the ice seems unsafe, the fisherman crosses it quickly and securely to the fishing spot.

Ice-angling
A symbiosis of methods

For many years, ice fishing for pike led an obscure life. But since the end of the 1990s, this sport has mushroomed. Ice angling combines the best of old 'tip-up' ice-fishing with modern angling technique. Using three or four rods per person, a couple of fishermen can quickly and effectively fish out hot spots, along cliffs and reed edges, or over shallows and vegetated areas with baitfish.

Equipment
Rod

The perfect rod for ice angling is hard to find in shops. Therefore, devotees make their own from the shortest, softest models of boat rods. The blade is cut just below the ferrule and inserted in the handle. This gives a relatively soft two-part rod of around one meter. It needs to be short, so that the fish can be reached in the landing phase. It should also be tough, to tolerate a fishing day's many movements or to be thrown on the ice at the height of the fight. Glass-fiber blades are thus better than carbon fiber. A soft blade is essential to avoid risking line breakage, when the fish makes strong rushes only a few meters from a fisherman standing stiffly on the ice.

Reel

Both multiplier reels and spinning reels are used. A multi-reel is set to release line as easily as possible, with no risk of back-lash. A tangle on the spool when the rod is lying on the ice and the fisherman is fifty meters away does not help matters. Many a fisherman has seen the equipment pulled away over the ice and disappear into the hole with a splash. For spinning, a baitrunner reel is preferable, since it can be free-coupled with a closed bail to avoid the risk of tangle.

Line

The line should be at least 0.45 mm (0.02 in) thick, and of nylon, to withstand wear against the ice edge while playing, and to reduce the risk of line breakage.

Rod holder and bite indicator "Feather"

An angling-gear feather holds the baitfish at the right depth and serves as a bite indicator. It is attached to the angling gear that sits on the ice as usual, and some small improvements can make it perfect. Near the top sits a flat red plastic plate, or a red-painted cork, as a visual indicator. If this is replaced with a red-painted ping-pong ball, it is easy to see from all directions. A piece of silicon tube threaded over the outermost tip, where the line is clamped on, decreases the risk of damage to the line. An eel-bell near the top is a fine acoustic indicator, easy to hear across the ice when a fish bites or the baitfish swims around as a big pike eyes it in the depths.

End tackle

The end tackle is simple. On the line above the leader is threaded a lead shot of 10–15 g (0.5 oz), enough to keep the baitfish at the proper depth, but not so heavy as to prevent it from swimming around attractively. The leader may be the same as for angling in open water: multi-strand wire material such as Drennan Sevenstrand, at least 40 cm (1,2 ft) long, with one or two thin treble hooks of size 6–8. The ideal is a 'semi-barbless' hook model, which can be replaced with ordinary models where the barb is squeezed in toward the shaft with pliers.

Right: Drill a series of holes, pull the equipment sledge along them, and rig rod after rod until you are done.
Far right: An echo sounder shows both the water depth and the locations of baitfish.

Far left: Ready to lower the baitfish.

Middle: The baitfish is sent down and the line is wound a few turns on a ring at the signal flag.

Above: Ready for bites. With one or two eel-bells on the signal flag, the bite can be seen and heard far across the ice.

Bait
Live

Roach is the classic bait, partly since it is easier to obtain, but also because it is a good bait. If correctly attached – with a treble hook in the back, or else one in the back and one in a breast fin – it will stay alive long and swim temptingly down below. Other baits also work, of course. Perch is superb in some waters, but worse in others. Live herring are excellent. A small aquarium net is fine for catching the fish in a bucket, and a sizable ice scoop will keep the hole free from ice.

Dead

Dead baitfish can be used, but are worse. At a guess, fat fish with a strong scent – such as herring and mackerel – should be better than, for example, roach.

Fishing depth

As a little boy, I followed my father in winter for ice fishing, and learned from the experts that roach should hang at the bottom, between half a meter and one meter up. Today's ice-anglers do not obey the old rule. Certainly, fish are also taken at the bottom, but often it is better to fish just under the ice. Especially towards evening, pike rise higher in the water to hunt.

Manual sounding

Sounding out the right depth is achieved by lowering the tackle until the line slackens. Then it is raised by the leader length plus the distance from the bottom that the bait will fish. If the bait is to hang under the ice, the tackle is let down so that the lead shot is just below the ice edge.

Echo sounder

An echo sounder increases the chances of finding fish. It is used both for fast and effective sounding, and to look for schools of baitfish.

Technique

Once the bait roach is lowered, the rod can be laid on the angling gear's spool or on the ice. If there is no snow, the rod should lie 5–6 m (15 ft) from the hole, as a fisherman who approaches the hole after a bite may frighten the pike.

The strike

The strike is made immediately if the fish pulls line. Otherwise, the line can be held carefully between your fingers to feel for movements. If any occur, strike fast.

Playing

After the strike, stay cool and give the fish time to tire out. Americans have a long tradition of ice fishing for big ones, and keep the drag brake set loosely to minimize risks. Instead, they brake with a finger on the spool when the fish rushes or line is to be pumped in.

Time

Ice angling is best under the first snow-free ice when the hunting light is good, and during the spring when the fish gather near spawning sites.

Left:
By gripping it under the gill arch toward the jaw, a pike is pulled up through the hole.

Right: *With long forceps, the hook is easily removed even if it sits some way inside the mouth. If the fish is to be released, it may best be left hanging in the hole while the hook is loosened.*

Perch and pikeperch
Float angling for perch

In lakes

Float angling with small baitfish is a classic summer pleasure. The tackle is the same as for ordinary pike angling, except that it must be more flexible and without a steel leader. A gliding float that allows rapid depth adjustment and can carry 5–10 g (0.2-0.4 oz) is adequate. Use nylon instead of steel for the leader, around 0.25 mm (0.01 in) thick, or a leader of Kevlar where the risk of a pike biting is great.

Hook, bait and rod

A broad-gap single hook, size 2–6, is best. Attach a roach, minnow, bleak or the like, 6–12 cm (2-5 in) long, by its upper lip or in front of the tail fin. If really big perch are the quarry, exchange the single hook for a thin-wire treble hook of size 6–8 for quick strikes, and use a baitfish around 15 cm (6 in) long. The best rods have soft action so that the baitfish is not pulled loose in the cast. Length should be 9–10 feet (3 m) for boat fishing and 12–13 feet (3.5–4 m) if fishing from land.

Opposite top: All that is needed for summer perch angling with small bait-fish. A gliding float for still waters, an Avon float for waterways with strong current, single hooks with a broad gap in sizes 4–6, and sinkers.
Opposite bottom: The pikeperch angler's accessory box: sliding floats that take 10–20 g (0.35-0.7 oz), sinkers of various weights for both float angling and bottom angling, swivels and snaps, single hooks for small bottom-angled baits, treble hooks of sizes 6–8, and leader material.

Reward for perch angling with roach – a perch weighing over a kilogram.

Tactics

Perch are mobile. If they do not bite within 20–30 minutes, try the next spot. Normally the bait is fished just over the bottom, but sometimes the perch are hunting and the baitfish struggle at the surface. Then the tackle should be raised to a meter below the surface. The bites are distinct and the float often disappears with a plop.

Flowing waters

In a waterway the tackle must drift with the current, keeping the baitfish just over the bottom. Brake its drift now and then. In late autumn and early winter, a better bait is often an earthworm or caterpillar under an Avon float (see the section on float angling). A large worm goes on a single hook of size 2–4, or some caterpillars on size 4–6.

Bottom angling for perch
Tackle

From autumn through spring, bottom angling is usually most effective. The simplest tackle is a paternoster, with a hook leader of 0.5–1 m (1,5-3 ft) and a sinker leader of 15–40 cm (6-15 in). The rod should be a quivertip of 11–12 feet (3–3.5 m).

Bait

Good baits are worms or baitfish up to 10–12 cm (4 in) long, rigged as above.

Tactics

Active fish are best. The hot area is fished by casting the bait and letting it lie for between half a minute and a few minutes, before pulling it in 0.5–1 m (1,5-3 ft).

Place
Lakes

In lakes there are perch over free bottoms, along submerged cliffs, near sunken trees, and at inlets or outlets. Bundles of brushwood are classic places for perch angling – artificial fishing spots created by sinking bushes in a place with an adequate depth of 3–6 m (10-20 ft). Small fish collect there and attract perch.

In summer, the right spots are where the wind blows best. It, too, draws small fish that attract perch. In spring, the fishing is hot at the spawning areas of perch. They may lie at a stream mouth, a pile of brushwood, or other spots where branches and rubbish are on the bottom, in which the fish can fasten their roe. During early spring, autumn and winter, perch can also be found over flat clay bottoms, often at depths over 6 m (20 ft).

An echo sounder makes it easier to find places with the right bottom structure and baitfish.

Streams

In flowing waters, perch occur within and near backwaters, behind sunken trees, in patches of vegetation and the like. The harder the current, the denser the perch hold in backwaters. Where no clear backwater exists, they hold in the weakest part of the current, at the inside of a curve or where the stream widens.

Streams and rivers that empty into the sea are especially good. They provide overwintering places for brackish-water perch. The fish run up the streams in late autumn and stay until spawning is finished, whereupon they migrate out to eat themselves fat.

Time

In summer, the best times are dawn and the last hours of daylight, but perch fishing offers several periods of biting during the day. Afternoon becomes ever better, the colder the water is. During winter, the only such period may come in the middle of the day.

Pikeperch

Both live and dead bait are taken by pikeperch. Besides the method for live bait, bottom-angling techniques with dead baitfish are therefore also useful. They range from free-line fishing, where the tackle is only a leader and the bait provides casting weight, to sliding tackle and other bottom-angling techniques for pike.

Leader

Pikeperch are wary of thick leaders, so it is better to use 0.40 mm nylon or modern super-flexible steel material – such as Drennan soft strand wire, or Kevlar if there is much risk of pike biting.

Top: A missed bite by a perch leaves its mark: the baitfish has only lost scales, without the characteristic wounds from pike teeth. With baits of this size, a treble hook of size 6–8 is better for fast, secure strikes.

Bottom: Pikeperch are sensitive to stiff leader materials. As they have gripping teeth, a leader can be of nylon or modern flexible 'clad' steel wire.

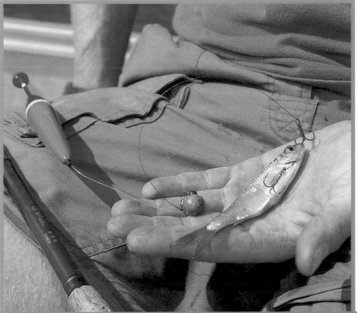

Place

In connection with spring spawning, pikeperch are found near spawning sites on free-lying stony ground, at cliffs with hard bottoms, or below migration obstacles in waterways that the fish run up in. During summer the fish are harder to locate, but usually hold near some kind of change in depth.

Time

Pikeperch are active at night, and then often swim near the surface. But in both early summer and autumn, the daytime fishing can match the angling by dark.

Handling

Fish that are returned to the water must always be handled carefully, and this is especially important with the sensitive pikeperch. Preferably, loosen the hooks with the fish still in the water, when lying in the net, for example. If the fish has to be lifted into the boat or up on land, do so briefly – otherwise the creature will not recover.

Eel

Eels are surrounded by mystery, tension and power. The eel that lies before you in a dark, dripping net may have begun its life fifteen years ago in the Sargasso Sea amid the Atlantic. Like a little transparent monster, perhaps it drifted with the current to a continental coast and, transformed into a thin miniature of your dream eel, took a waterway up to a fishing paradise.

Equipment and tackle
Rod

An eel is incredibly strong and can instantly set itself immovably on the bottom. Without hard and determined strikes, followed by a hefty left, the fight can be lost there. So the rod needs strength and length to lift the fish directly at the strike. A carp rod of 12 feet (3.5 m) is perfect.

Reel and bite indicator

A spinning reel is best, ideally with a monkey-climber as a bite indicator, and an open bail so that the fish can take line freely. Eels are often so sensitive to resistance that you cannot use a baitrunner, as they would let go of the bait.

A simple bite-indicating alternative is to hang a big tin can below the reel, and lay some coins on the spool after opening the bail.

Tackle

Sliding bottom angling is usually most effective. Use a sinker of 20–40 g (0.7-1,5 oz) on a swivel with snap, so that the weight can be altered according to the conditions – as well as a plastic bead before the leader's swivel to protect the knot.

Leader

One of the greatest eel-fishing experts of all time, the late John Sidley from England, believed that a steel leader is essential. In my experience, it happens very seldom that an eel damages a 0.35 mm (0.01 in) nylon leader seriously. But when fishing in waters where every fish is a giant, it may be smartest to use a steel leader anyway. Imagine if a dream fish should disappear into the depths because of a 'sawed-off' leader after many fishless nights.

Prepare your leaders by daylight. It is easier to tie on a new

With a quick strike, the hook often sits in the corner of the eel's mouth.

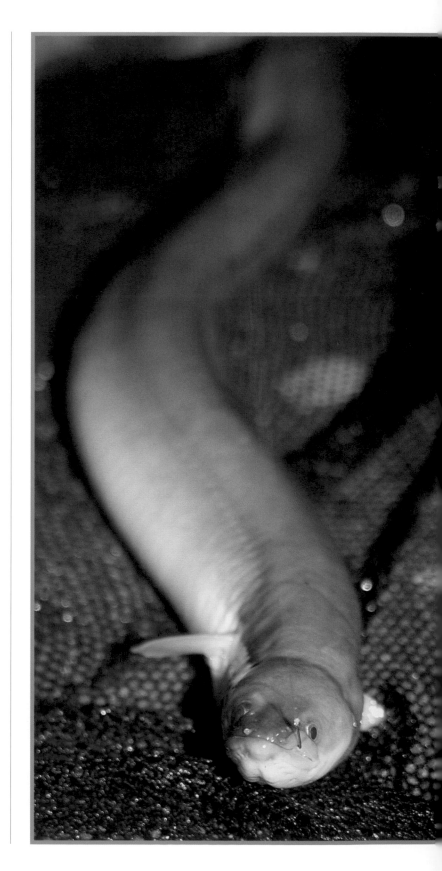

Baitfish for eel is tackled on most simply by drawing the leader through the fish with a bait needle.
Be careful that the bait does not hide the hook – the tip should be free for optimum penetration.

leader in the dark than to put one together with a torch between your teeth.

Hook

A hook with a broad gap is best. For earthworms, size 2–4 is adequate, the smaller for one worm and the bigger for several. The same sizes suit baitfish and shrimp. With shrimp, an eel is best caught if the hook sits in the middle of the bait, at a ninety-degree angle.

Bait
Worms

Earthworms are my first choice, but I often fish on a rod with fish or pieces of fish as a test, and to have a bait that is undis-turbed by small fish. I pinch off a bit of the earthworm to release a little extra aromatic juice.

Baitfish

Besides roach, bleak and small perch, smelt is a good bait as it has a strong, pickle-like smell.

Baitfish are normally best when very fresh. Preferably you should bring small live roaches and bleak in a bucket, and knock them on the head a second before putting them on the hook.

Shrimp

In marine or brackish waters, shrimp tend to be best. When the fishing is done in a harbor, shrimp remains and other rub-bish are thrown into the water to attract eels.

Tactics

Eels have the fishing world's sharpest sense of smell. So change the bait often, at least once per half hour. New bait smells stronger, attracts better and catches more fish.

Pull in the bait by half a meter to one meter after the cast, where the bottom allows it, so as to create a smelly trail. With longer 'hot bottoms' the bait is best fished by pulling it in at intervals of five to ten minutes. Often the bite comes just after a pull.

Place
Stationary fishing

Harbors are good because of the natural prebaiting that their rubbish provides. In marine waters, the criteria are different. The biggest eels can be found in waters with sparse stocks – far up in a system of waterways, or in lakes with migration obstacles that make it hard for eels to get there. In dense stocks of eel, few specimens become large. The strongest ones wander far from their relatives, to grow big without a hard fight for food.

Migrating eels

Things are different when fishing for migrating eel. In spring and late summer, the large females start the journey back to their birthplace. Then the fishing is best at strategic places where they have to pass by – at promontories, or near outlets in the lower parts of extensive waterway systems.

Time

Eel fishing is best by dark, in the hours after dusk and until midnight. The best time of year is usually September, but eels can be caught throughout the summer half-year.

Last words

The dilemma for an eel-fishing lover is that eels are becoming ever more rare. Enjoy your eel fishing and the darkness, the excitement, the fish's raw strength – but release the big ones. There are not many left, and the fewer they get, the more our future stocks and eel fishing depend on some of them returning to the water and spawning. A single two-kilogram eel can produce 20 million eggs, which gives a perspective on what one released fish may mean for the future.

Above:
*Even small ponds with
no clear inlet or outlet
can contain big eels.*

Left:
*Shrimp should be tack-
led on with the hook
through the middle of
the bend. A hook at
ninety degrees will
penetrate best.*

Burbot

Fishing by dark is a feature common to burbot and eel angling. But there are important differences, such as the fish's behavior when it takes the bait, and the fact that burbot fishing belongs to the cold part of the year.

Equipment and tackle
Rod and reel

A rod at least 10 feet (3 m) long, for casting weights from 35–40 g (1.5 oz), and a spinning reel, preferably with a baitrunner, using 0.30–0.40 mm (0.01 in) line, make a good basis.

Tackle and sinker

Burbot often gobble the bait fast. Fishing with sliding tackle can therefore yield deeply hooked fish, since the bite is not registered quickly enough. Frequently it is better to fish with a fixed sinker, or bolt tackle. To ensure that the fish does not swallow without the bite being noticed, the leader must be short, 20–30 cm (1 ft). The sinker needs to be at least 50 g (2 oz) if the bolt effect is to work.

Hook

In order to expose the hook tip for penetration when the fish takes the bait in its mouth, a large hook is required. A single hook of size 2–4/0, depending on the bait's size, will do. Circle hooks are best, as they usually hook the fish in the corner of the jaw. For a small piece of fish, hook size 2–1/0 is used, and 1/0 – 4/0 for a whole fish.

Bait

Best is smelt, which outclass other baits in places where they occur naturally. Other good baits are strong-smelling fish such as herring, or shrimp and earthworms. Fish baits and shrimp are preferable, since they attract larger fish compared with earthworms, which can be swallowed by small burbot as well as roach and perch.

Place
Lake

In lakes, burbot are found near deeper areas, 15–20 m (65 ft) being popular. Promontories, shallows, or cliffs with hard bottom, stones, sand or, in some cases, hard clay, are normally best. But when burbot hunt, they come near

Above: One way to increase the tackle's attractiveness is to rig a starlight with a couple of pieces of rigtub near the hook.
Opposite: Burbot fishing is very sensitive to fishing pressure. Whoever wants to enjoy continued good fishing releases the big ones.

land, so it can pay to use short casts of 10–15 m (45 ft)

Flowing waters

In rivers and streams, the most reliable holding places are in backwaters. The stronger the current, the more concentrated the fish are. Along promontories or sharp bends, in deep holes, behind boulder and bridge pillars – these are typical spots.

Power-plant channels can hold plenty of fish. There they are 'chummed' by fish that have been sucked into the turbines. Moreover, some current obstacle is usually there for the fish to linger behind.

Time

Burbot are most active during the winter half-year. From November until the ice forms (where it does so) normally counts as best. If there is open water at the spawning grounds, during the spawning period from January to March, it is even hotter. Spawning occurs on hard bottoms with ample current, at promontories or on free-lying ground.

Burbot are nocturnal. The best times tend to be from dusk onward for a couple of hours.

Sheatfish

Fishing for European sheatfish, which can weigh over 100 kg (200 lb), is the heavyweight challenge of angling. Sheatfish occur naturally in most of the river systems in Eastern Europe, and implantations have established the fish in most of the larger Southern European rivers. When hunting sheatfish, there are chances of catching a specimen bigger than the fisherman.

Drum-fishing

Sheatfish are caught with bottom and float angling by the methods that have been described for pike. But a special kind of angling developed for sheatfish is ever more predominant: 'drum-fishing'.

A drum or jerry can is attached to a stone with a strong line, so that it floats at the surface where the fisherman wants to present the bait. One rows out with the tackle ready – a leader with a baitfish – and ties it to the drum with a 'crack-line' 2–3 m (9 ft) long. Then one rows back and tenses up the line, so that it hangs over the water surface. The rod is placed in a holder pointing upward. Now the baitfish works in the surface and just below it. When a sheatfish bites, the crack-line is torn off, the hook is dug in by the resistance, and the fisherman grabs the rod to dig it in further.

The drilling is usually done from a boat, as this lessens the risk of the fish getting caught in submerged trees, roots or the like.

Equipment
Rod

The rods must be very strong, 9–11 feet (2.5–3.5 m) long, with deep action that allows them to be tensed in an arc against the drum. Glass-fiber rods are better than carbon-fiber ones, since they are more durable and have softer action. This is needed because the fish delivers long blows and may let go if they create slack line.

Reel and line

Multiplier reels that take at least 250–300 m (900 ft), and 0.55 mm (0.02 in) line, are required. The fishing may be done at distances of around and above 100 m (300 ft), and there must be extra line for the fish's long rushes.

The line should be of the 'braided super-line' type in

The sheatfish is secured on a stringer.

strengths of 30–70 kg (60-150 lb), depending on how much rubbish is in the water that the fish can get caught in.

Hook, leader and crack-line

Both broad-gap single and treble hooks are used, in sizes from 1/0 to 14/0, depending on the fish's size. The treble hooks are of sizes 1/0–4/0, and the single hooks of sizes 4/0–14/0. For leaders, the choice is Kevlar of strength 50–100 kg (100-200 lb). The hooks are knotted to the leader so that one can be fastened in the baitfish's back at the dorsal fin, and one in the upper lip or at a breast fin, since the bite comes from below. The leader's length should be 50–100 cm (1.5-3 ft) and it is tied to a strong swivel, rated at about 100 kg (200 lb), to which the crack-line can also be tied.

The crack-line must have the right strength to break when the sheatfish attacks the bait, but not so weak that the hook fails to penetrate. Dacron of 5-7 kg (10–15 lb) is adequate.

Bite indicator

The reel is set with a click or a loose brake. A bite indicator with an alarm that sounds when the rod bends back is used as a complement.

Bait

Live bait is superior to dead bait, and must be as lively as possible. In river fishing, it is important to check often that no rubbish has snagged on the leader and hinders the baitfish's movements.

Carp, bream, crucian carp, large roach, and eel, with weights from half a kilo to two kilos, are good bait.

Place
Flowing waters

The fish hold in deep holes and backwaters, stealing into shallower areas at night to hunt. Good fishing places are at the edges between strong and weak currents, on the insides of curves, outside shallow areas with vegetation, and in clean backwaters.

Lakes

Drum-fishing is most popular in flowing waterways, but also works in lakes. Good spots are near shallow vegetated coves, where deep edges reach up, at belts of plants and the like.

Time

Sheatfishing is best during the summer half-year, but the ideal periods in southern rivers are March–April and September–October.

Fishing is better by night than by day. During sixteen days of fishing on the Ebro in Spain, three fishermen caught 44 sheatfish, only one of them by daylight.

Conditions

The sheatfish relies mainly on other senses than its sight when hunting – among others, its long feelers. A baitfish can be 'fake-attacked' several times before the sheatfish takes it properly. Perhaps this is why the fishing can improve greatly when the water is really murky.

After periods of drought, heavy rain and lightning can get the fish moving. The reason is undoubtedly that the water is stirred up, and because everything edible is washed into the rivers. As usual, however, there are differing opinions; some believe that the fishing is terrible when it rains.

Right: *The rig for livebaiting a large bream on the surface.*
Far right: *Although the sheatfish mouth is big enough it is not always easy to find a hookhold.*

North America

Modern angling has long since conquered Europe. But new challenges arise. The North American continent is a dreamland for anglers. And while American journals such as 'In-Fisherman' have occasionally discussed European techniques, American anglers have only scratched the surface of the possibilities that exist.

Carp

Almost the entire continent offers such fishing as can hardly be imagined by European carp anglers. From southern Canada to the southernmost American states, there are innumerable waters with large stocks of carp. And these are not tiny fish. In rivers, dammed-up reservoirs, and natural lakes, there are plenty of sizable fish – golden, turbocharged mountain carp.

In the USA, carp are widely regarded as vermin. Several states forbid the releasing of carp once they are hooked. In places where angling is unknown, hunting with bows and arrows for carp and other 'rough fish' is a popular amusement.

Exceptions occur, though. One pioneer is Bernie Haines, originally from England but a many-year resident of Houston, Texas. From April to October, he guides European carp-fishing guests on tours along the powerful St. Lawrence River at the border between the USA and Canada.

Alligator gar

Another species of low repute in the USA is the alligator gar. But many European anglers would presumably give an arm or leg to catch one. This is a primitive fish with more than seventy million years behind it, and can weigh over 150 kilograms. Looking like a cross between a crocodile and a monster pike, it leaps during the fight, and has an armored jaw that makes it almost impossible to hook. It is one of the sportfishing world's greatest challenges, living in the southern states' swamps, rivers and reservoirs.

Other species

Many of the southern rivers have Chinese carp weighing over 30 kg (60 lb). Giants, too, are the two 'buffalo' species, of which the 'smallmouth buffalo' is biggest. This carp-like fish can reach weights of around 50 kg (100 lb). Also here are three species of large-grown sheatfish that, apart from their barbels and way of life, are not very reminiscent of European sheatfish.

Above: A small example of the 'bluecat', caught on a bait intended for carp in a southerly lake in Texas. Also in North America are two other large sheatfish species, the 'channelcat' and 'yellowcat'. Both the blue and yellow ones reach weights of around 50 kg (110 lb).

Opposite:
Top: The carp that swim in North American rivers are golden power-packs that have nothing in common with their European cousins except appearance and appetite.
Bottom: This is considered a 'rough fish' by many American fishermen.

Index